WARRIORS
and
WITCHES
and
DAMN
REBEL BITCHES

SCOTTISH WOMEN
TO LIVE YOUR LIFE BY

MAIRI KIDD

BLACK & WHITE PUBLISHING

First published 2019
by Black & White Publishing Ltd
Nautical House, 104 Commercial Street
Edinburgh, EH6 6NF

3 5 7 9 10 8 6 4 2   20 21 22 23
Reprinted 2020

ISBN: 978 1 78530 236 7

Sources for the quote(s) on:
p.8 is taken from 'Verba Scáthaige' by P. L. Henry, in *Celtica 21* (1990), p.200.
p.64 is taken from 'Clemency Ealasaid' by Naomi Mitchison, in *The Bull Calves*
  (1947), preface.
p.78 is taken from Belle Stewart recorded by Henderson et al., School of Scottish
  Studies SA1977.159.1.
p.152 is taken from Donald MacIntyre recorded by Campbell and MacLean,
  School of Scottish Studies SA1952.143.2.
p.200 is taken from *North to the Rime-ringed Sun* by Isobel Wylie Hutchison
  (1934), p.151.

A CIP catalogue record for this book is available from the British Library.

Layout by Richard Budd Design
Printed and bound by Grafički Zavod Hrvatske, Croatia

CONTENTS

WITCHES

DAMN REBEL BITCHES

For Kirsty MacDonald –
living embodiment of
why friends matter,
how much women can face without breaking
and why it's best not to get involved with dickheads.

INTRODUCTION

This book begins with a challenge. Let's say you have a five-year-old daughter growing up in Scotland in 2019. Where might you turn for examples of Scottish women to inspire her?

In the modern era, you'd have it relatively easy. From politicians to actresses, artists to writers and sportswomen to singers, modern-day Scotland has produced any number of confident, successful women offering great examples to any little girl.

Go back a little further, though, and you might begin to struggle. You certainly couldn't point your daughter to traditional indicators of status such as public monuments – there are almost no statues of women in Scotland. Our capital Edinburgh groans under the weight of hundreds of statues of men and precisely three of women, one whom is Queen Victoria and another an anonymous figure symbolising victims of apartheid. Only the statue of Helen Crummy outside Craigmillar Library on the eastern outskirts of the city immortalises a named woman of Scotland, a heroine of community arts provision who transformed her local area through dedication and sheer hard work. By contrast, Edinburgh boasts statues of several animals – the pampered pooches of Walter Scott, Robert Louis Stevenson and James Clerk Maxwell, Polish/Scottish war bear Wojtek, Greyfriars Bobby, a horse called Copenhagen and even a dog called Bum. This list makes it clear where women fall in the pecking order with sculptors and the commissioners of public art.

In the relative invisibility of the women of our past, Scotland is not unusual. Until quite recently, a person reading Western history could have been forgiven for believing that women didn't really exist at all. The world was largely run for men, by men, and history was written along these same principles. Occasional women do appear: when a queen consort produces an heir, or worse, fails in this task; very rarely when a king dies with no male heir and his daughter inherits; when a pretender's wife or daughter is bartered as a hostage. These women are almost exclusively royal, or at least noble or aristocratic, and records tend to treat them briefly at best and unkindly at worst. As regards the 'ordinary' women of any given country – i.e. the vast majority – history is generally silent. In fairness, it is often silent too in regards to the lives of 'ordinary' men. In Scotland's case this challenge is compounded by our complex constitutional history and our rich linguistic heritage, which many of us are ill-equipped to navigate.

If you did decide to brave Scotland's archives – of which we boast many, having a proud and lengthy legal tradition – you might discover an arresting fact. In our court records, the words and deeds of 'ordinary' Early Modern Scottish – and Scots-speaking – women are recorded unusually extensively. Sadly, these appear in the depositions and 'dittays' of witch trials and these women are victims of a terrifying persecution which has left them fighting for their lives. Others appear as accusers and witnesses for the prosecution. Thankfully, these accounts are far from a fair representation of the lived reality of our foremothers – surely we can do better.

This book doesn't aim to give a complete account of Scotland's women – such a thing would be impossible – but rather begins with the idea of that five-year-old living in Scotland today. What sort of world would we wish for her, and which women's stories could help inspire her towards it? And so here you will find a group of women selected for their wit, for their wisdom, and even for their wickedness, and some thoughts on the inspiration that a modern woman – whether young or old or in between – might take from their experience. Because the truth is, of course, that women have always made up roughly half of the people of the world, and women's experiences have always mattered, to women if not to men. Many of these stories cannot be found in traditional histories, but they are there in oral tradition, in exaggerated caricatures, monstrous exaggerations and idealised hagiographies hiding in the margins of history proper. This book does its fair share of reading between the lines, in English and in Gaelic and in Scots, in the margins and in the gaps. Hopefully you will forgive any errors in the reading that you find, and enjoy your time in the company of these Scottish sisters.

WARRIORS

WARRIORS

Slap on your war-paint, put 'em up and get set for a square go in the company of sisters from the earliest times in Scotland's history to the present day. Scottish women have never been afraid to get their hands dirty and, from pivotal actions in the Wars of Independence to life-saving healthcare in a context of modern mechanised warfare, they have battled terrible odds, stood up for what they believed was right, and changed the course of history.

These 'bonnie fechters' stood fearless and true to themselves – follow their example and you can, too.

"A mbeë eirr ōengaile,
arut·ossa ollgābud,
uathad fri h-éit n-imlebair.
Cotut- chaurith ·cēillfetar,
fortat- brágit ·bibsatar . . .

Ferba do breig braitfiter,
brāgit do- thuaith ·tithsitir . . ."

"When you are a peerless champion,
great peril awaits you,
alone against the vast herd.
Chosen warriors will be set against you,
necks will be broken by you . . .

Cows will be carried off from your hill,
    captives will be forfeited by your people . . ."

SGÀTHACH USING HER GIFT OF
IMBAS FOROSNAI ~ VISIONARY POETIC TRANCE ~ TO TELL
CÙ CHULAINN'S FUTURE (RECONSTRUCTION OF A LOST
8TH~CENTURY TEXT FROM LATER SOURCES BY P. L. HENRY)

SGÀTHACH

WARRIOR AND TEACHER

The ruins of Dùn Sgàthaich cling to an offshore rock in Sleat, on the southern tip of Skye. In the Middle Ages the castle was a stronghold of Clan Donald of Sleat but, in a world of buildings named after men from the Middle Ages onwards, it's refreshing to realise that Dùn Sgàthaich commemorates an earlier era and a woman to boot. She was Sgàthach – Shadowy One – and she was a legendary warrior.

When the great Ulster hero, Cù Chulainn, sought to marry, his sweetheart Emer's father refused his permission until Cù Chulainn had trained in Scotland with Sgàthach. This condition was designed to ensure the marriage never happened – Sgàthach's castle was so difficult to find, so impregnable, and her training so mortally dangerous that few returned when they sought her out. Cù Chulainn found Dùn Sgàthaich, gained access and spent seven years there while Sgàthach taught him all of the arts of war. To him alone she taught the use of her *Gáe Bulg*, a fearsome barbed spear she threw with her foot and which had to be cut out of its victim. She gave the *Gáe Bulg* to Cù Chulainn, who used it with terrible success for the rest of his life.

Before he left Sgàthach's castle, Cù Chulainn fought by her side and helped her vanquish her rival, Aoife.

Sgàthach appears in the Ulster Cycle, one of the four great branches of Irish mythology. The texts that survive today date from the 1400s, but there are glimpses in these manuscripts of earlier language structures suggesting that the originals of the stories are very much older. The action is set around 200 to

400 AD. Did Sgàthach really exist in Scotland at this time? Probably not, but her story offers us a tantalising glimpse of a society that did not think strong, independent warrior women outlandish.

LIVE YOUR LIFE BY SGÀTHACH

Real or not, you could do worse than start with Sgàthach as an indomitable, gutsy example to us all – a heroine who knew her own worth. Sgàthach had no time for mediocrity – she would only train the best warriors, and she ensured they were the best by setting serious tests for them to pass before they could even gain access to her school. Take a leaf out of Sgàthach's book to get on in the world. Don't let yourself be spoken over, patronised or talked down to, at work or in your relationships. Decide to be the very best you can be, and take the time to allow yourself to achieve that. At work, grab on to training opportunities, mentorships and chances to step up. You deserve it and you can do it. We can all be our own worst enemies, listening to those insidious little voices in our head that say we can't. Sgàthach evidently didn't listen to hers, and neither should you.

DEVORGILLA OF GALLOWAY
RELIGIOUS PATRON

Devorgilla was born around 1210 to Alan, Lord of Galloway and his second wife Margaret of Huntington. If her name looks a bit of a mouthful, it's actually a Latinised version around half the length of her original Gaelic name Dearbhfhorghaill. Looking for baby name inspiration? In modern Gaelic this riot of consonants is often equated to 'Dorothy'.

Devorgilla's dad was one of the most powerful lords in Scotland at the time, and her grandfather on her mother's side was the youngest brother of not one but two kings of Scotland – Malcolm IV and William the Lion. This meant that Devorgilla had a reasonably strong claim to the Scottish throne. In an era in which life often came to an early and bloody end – especially for those with a claim to the Scottish throne – 'reasonably strong' was often good enough.

In 1223 Devorgilla married John, Baron de Balliol, whose family held Barnard Castle in County Durham. She was around thirteen years old. This was not an uncommon age for betrothal and marriage at a time when life was short, questionable as it may seem today.

Alan of Galloway died in 1234, survived by three legitimate daughters and one illegitimate son. The son might have inherited under local Gaelic custom, but King Alexander II perhaps recognised the danger that a strong leader in Galloway posed to his rule. The three daughters were all married to powerful Anglo-Norman lords and therefore looked the easier bet to control, especially if they had only a portion of Galloway's wealth each. And so Galloway was divided three ways, giving Devorgilla substantial lands and wealth in her own right.

Devorgilla and John had nine children and the marriage was evidently a happy one, if somewhat dramatic; when John died in 1269, Devorgilla had his heart embalmed and placed in an ivory and silver casket so she could she keep it with her for the rest of her life. She also founded a Cistercian Abbey in Galloway in her husband's memory.

A few years before his death, John de Balliol lost a land dispute with the Bishop of Durham and was required to found a college for the poor at Oxford University as penance. His finances were not up to the task; Devorgilla had to step in after his death to confirm the foundation of Balliol College, and to make provisions for its financing and statutes. The college retains the Balliol name to the present day, its history students have a society called after Devorgilla and, while it was slow to admit female students, today it is host to an annual series of seminars by female academics named in Devorgilla's honour.

Devorgilla was buried beside her husband – still clutching his embalmed heart – at the new abbey she had founded. After her death her fourth and youngest son John Balliol asserted his claim to the throne of Scotland through his mother's line. In 1292 he became John I, King of Scots. John was, in effect, a puppet king controlled by Edward I of England, and history remembers him unkindly as 'Toom Tabard', or Empty Jacket. His mother's energy and devotion, on the other hand, are remembered more kindly, and the ruins of the abbey she founded are known to this day as 'Sweetheart Abbey' in recognition of her slightly obsessive love for her husband and her more conventional love of God.

"Mulier magna opibus et praediis tam in Anglia quam in Scotia; sed multo major ingenuitate cordis . . ."

"a woman much endowed with money and lands in England and in Scotland; she had a much richer endowment in the nobility of her heart . . ."

THE LANERCOST CHRONICLE RECORDS
THE LIFE AND DEATH OF DEVORGILLA

LIVE YOUR LIFE BY DEVORGILLA

While Devorgilla is best remembered for grand and – let's be honest – slightly repulsive romantic gestures, she was very much in charge of her own destiny because she was also very much in charge of her own finances. For all that most of us can't expect to inherit a third of a lordship to keep us in funds, there's a lesson in there that managing your money actively is a very good thing to do. In Devorgilla's case there was a LOT of work involved – she's on record as fighting a large number of legal cases over her own and her husband's estates – but to be a modern lady of substance you need to do a bit of active management too. Control that spending by stepping away from the net when you've had a glass of wine and cutting up your credit cards if you tend to spend your salary before you've earned it. Try to save a little every month, shop savvy – the planet will thank you as well as your finances – and switch deals on the regular to save on your power, your mortgage and any loans or cards you use. Don't spend the money on ivory and silver receptacles for your loved one's body parts, though, that's mental. If you have spare funds, you might honour Devorgilla by donating to a transplant or heart disease charity, and make sure you carry a donor card so that your body parts can share their true value after your death.

AGNES RANDOLPH
COUNTESS OF DUNBAR

Black-haired, black-eyed Agnes was born around 1312 to Thomas Randolph, Early of Moray and Isabel Stewart of the Stewarts of Bonkyll. Feistiness ran in the blood; on both sides the family were active in resisting English forces in the Wars of Independence.

In 1324 Agnes married Patrick, Earl of Dunbar and March and governor of Berwick. In 1333 Berwick was occupied by Edward I's forces and Patrick joined the English side. In return Agnes and Patrick were granted English lands and permission to build up the defences of Dunbar Castle. Once this work was done, Patrick switched sides back to Scotland and joined the fight.

During the Wars of Independence some noblemen changed sides as often as most of us change our pants, but clearly Patrick's actions rankled with England. In 1338 he was away from home and William Montague, Earl of Salisbury, decided to lay siege to Dunbar Castle. A force of 20,000 men gathered outside the walls. Inside were Lady Agnes, her servants and a few guards. The odds must have seemed entirely in Salisbury's favour, huh? But he hadn't reckoned on Agnes.

First Salisbury tried to break down the castle's defences by catapulting lead shot and boulders against the walls. The walls held. Between bombardments, Lady Agnes had her maidservants step out to dust off the tops of the walls with their white headscarves. She was owning this one already.

Next Salisbury turned to his 'sow' – a wooden tower to help his men climb the castle walls. Agnes had her guards drop one of Salisbury's own boulders on the tower and crushed it to pieces.

Salisbury gave up on force and tried cunning. He bribed the guard on the gate to leave the gate open. The guard took the money and told Agnes of the plan. As soon as the first Englishman ran into the castle, Agnes dropped the gate and trapped him inside. She had hoped to catch Salisbury himself, but one of his men had pushed ahead. 'Farewell, Montague,' Agnes called down. 'I intended that you should have supped with us, and assist us in defending the castle against the English.'

It seems safe to assume that Salisbury was becoming quite frustrated by this point. He brought Agnes's brother to Dunbar and threatened to hang him in view of the castle. Lovely, bluffed Agnes; with her brother out of the way, she would be one step closer to his land and titles. She wasn't really in line to succeed, but the bluff worked and who knows? She wouldn't be the first sister to enjoy a bit of revenge on her brother for childhood teasing.

In the end, the only option left to Salisbury was to starve Agnes and her people out. But Ramsay of Dalhousie and a force of forty men commandeered small boats and entered the castle by sea. Ramsay's men stormed out of the castle and forced Salisbury's men back to their camp.

Five months had passed and Salisbury had not taken the castle, although he had spent a fortune in the attempt. It was time to admit defeat. Agnes had held her house – with style.

"Of Scotland's King
I haud my house,
I pay him meat and fee,
And I will keep my
gude auld house,
and my house will
keep me."

AGNES RANDOLPH
FACES AN ENGLISH SIEGE
1338

LIVE YOUR LIFE BY AGNES

Agnes knew the importance of a house and she wasn't giving hers up for anyone. Make sure you have your own house in order, literally and metaphorically. Your home gives you safety and security – never let anyone imperil that.

Never give up your own bank account or the management of your finances to someone else. You are responsible to you and however much or little you have, you need to manage it in your own best interests. If you co-own or co-rent, make sure your name is on the paperwork, especially if you are the carer of children. Keep a record of what you bring to any relationship, and what you pay into any common property during it. Any relationship can fail – ensure you have a sure and safe haven should it happen to you.

MARGARET WILSON

MARTYR

Margaret Wilson was the daughter of Gilbert Wilson, a successful farmer at Glenvernoch in Galloway. She was born in the second half of the 1600s, when Scotland was torn by religious conflict. Hold tight, this gets a bit technical . . .

Down in London, King Charles II had been restored to the throne in 1660, a little over a decade after his father Charles I had lost his head. The younger Charles may have been famous as a wig-wearing, fun-loving, mistress-impregnating fan of small floppy-eared dogs, but he also had strong opinions on religion when it suited him. He expressed these largely through an effort to ensure Scotland's church was administered by bishops. Bishops, you see, provide a handy conduit for power to the crown.

Many people in Scotland had other ideas. History is silent on their opinion on spaniels, but in religious terms they had a distinct preference for Presbyterian worship, i.e. more power to the people. They were known as Covenanters as they signed the National Covenant to make it clear they had no truck with bishops. They made their feelings especially clear on this in May 1679 when they assassinated James Sharp, the most powerful archbishop in the country.

Charles immediately got down to some serious religious repression. Entire communities were forced to sign the 'Abjuration Oath', or die. Many refused. The 1680s became known as the 'Killing Time'.

In Glenvernoch, Gilbert Wilson and his wife conformed, signed the Oath and worshipped in an Episcopalian establishment. Their children, Margaret, Thomas and Agnes, rebelled. Gilbert was held responsible for their non-attendance at church and was fined and forced to quarter government troops

"I wish the salvation of all men, but the damnation of none."

MARGARET WILSON
SPEAKS AT HER EXECUTION
1685

at his farm, suffering plunder and theft that was pretty much sanctioned by the authorities. Margaret, Agnes and Thomas fled to the hills, attending open-air services and meetings in other Covenanter homes.

When Charles II died in Feburary 1685, there was hope that the persecution of the Covenanters might end. Margaret and Agnes came down from the hills and went into Wigtown, where a local man betrayed them. The girls were taken prisoner and held with Margaret McLachlan, a widow in her sixties, who had been seized for the heinous act of praying wrong in her own home.

The two Margarets and Agnes were brought before a Commission of Greirson of Lag, Sheriff David Graham, Major Windram, Captain Strachan and Provost Coltrane of Wigtown, who were almost exactly as bad as they sound. The women were found guilty and sentenced to be 'tyed to palisades fixed in the sand, within the flood mark of the sea, and there to stand till the flood overflowed them and drowned them'. Gilbert Wilson managed to secure a reprieve for thirteen-year-old Agnes, at the then enormous cost of £100.

On 30 April 1685, a reprieve was issued in Edinburgh for Margaret Wilson, 18, and Margaret McLachlan, 63, but either it did not reach Wigtown or it didn't suit the Commission and was ignored. The women were taken out into the Bladnoch River on 11 May 1685 and tied to stakes at the mouth of Wigtown Bay. Margaret MacLachlan was tied deeper in the channel than Margaret Wilson in the hope that Margaret would witness the death of the older woman and relent. Instead, she seemed to take strength, singing and quoting from the Bible as the older woman died.

Records from the Kirk Session in Penninghame say that Margaret's head was held up from the water, and Major Windram offered her the chance to take the Oath of Abjuration again, but she refused, saying 'I am one of Christ's children; let me go'.

Tradition has it that many involved in the killing of the two Margarets later paid for their actions. An officer who held down Margaret McLachlan's head with his spear and joked that she should take another drink was cursed with an unquenchable thirst so that he could not pass a ditch or puddle without drinking. A constable who joked that the women danced webbed-footed around the stakes like crabs fathered a whole family of webbed-fingered children. Greirson of Lag is remembered in history as 'Cruel Lag' and the Commission more generally as 'five of the most vicious scoundrels in Scotland'.

LIVE YOUR LIFE BY MARGARET

In today's Scotland we don't have to die for our beliefs and we can be grateful for that. Poor Margaret did, but as she died she kept her wits about her and made some excellent speeches that have been preserved for the best part of four hundred years. Channel her example and you, too, can become an excellent public speaker. Follow these tips and you'll be fine.

- It's okay to be nervous. In many situations, nerves help us stay sharp. Learn to control your breathing and you can use nerves to your advantage. Another way to look at nervousness is as excitement.
- Remember that your audience want to be pleased. Start with an anecdote or arresting fact. Don't worry too much about making them laugh, but do make it personal if there's a way to incorporate personal detail that's appropriate. People are interested in people.
- Know your material, and make sure you have notes with you in the form you find most useful. Don't read from a script – boil what you need to say down to an outline that is as brief as you can get away with while still remembering the content.
- Don't be afraid of silence. Get comfortable before you start speaking, and if you need to pause to gather your thoughts for a second, don't worry.
- What's the worst that can happen? Unlike Margaret, you'll live to speak another day.

Oh, and don't avoid Wigtown. It's a lovely place, Scotland's first Book Town and home to a fantastic book festival every September. Definitely worth a visit at any time of year.

JEAN ARMOUR
WIFE AND MOTHER

History has done Jean Armour few favours. Described by Robert Burns's biographer Catherine Carswell as an 'unfeeling heifer', the woman who bore Burns nine children, stood by him through thick and thin and even raised the child of one of his mistresses has been generally dismissed as unsympathetic, unintelligent and largely undeserving of the love of her own husband.

Jean's family most certainly did not agree with this assessment; they thought Robert Burns no match at all for their pretty young daughter. When Jean first met him, hanging her laundry on a drying green in Mauchline in 1784, he had little but his wits to recommend him. His father had died, the family farm at Tarbolton had failed and he and his brother Gilbert had moved to Mossgiel where their struggles continued. He had a stoop and poor health thanks to hard labour on the farm since childhood, and while he had a handsome face and evident charm, he had already employed these to get his mother's servant Elizabeth Paton in the family way.

Jean, on the other hand, was the daughter of stonemason James Armour, one of Mauchline's most upstanding citizens. She was a pretty girl, considered one of the 'Belles' of the village, could read her Bible and had a beautiful singing voice. Although Jean chased Burns off on that first meeting – or at least, shooed his dog away from her washing – they inevitably met again and soon a courtship had begun. When, in 1786, Jean became pregnant, they made an informal marriage agreement. The story goes that Jean's father fainted in horror and had

"Our Robbie
should have had
twa wives."

JEAN ARMOUR
WRITES TO HER MOTHER
1793

to be revived by a 'cordial' (think a nice liqueur, not Apple and Blackcurrant).

Mrs Armour sent Jean off to Paisley in disgrace. But word had spread and soon both Burns and Jean were called before the Kirk to confess to their affair. In Burns's case, this meant making three appearances in church to do penance before he was given a certificate to say he was single again. For Jean, pregnant with twins, one imagines there was a bit more work involved.

It seems at this point that Burns considered that Jean had ended their marriage agreement and deserted him. His letters speak of his desire to find 'another wife' and before five minutes were up he had become involved with Mary Campbell, known as 'Highland Mary' in his poems. But when Mary died, Burns decided to emigrate to Jamaica and planned to publish a collection of poems to finance his voyage. Hearing word of this plan, James Armour issued a warrant against him and Burns holed up with his aunt until his book was published, transferring his property to his brother Gilbert to support Elizabeth Paton's child.

The book Burns published, the *Kilmarnock Edition*, was an instant success. Burns moved to Edinburgh for a time, where he was the toast of the town and where his flirtation with Agnes Maclehose began (see page 121). Jean had given birth to twins, Robert and Jean, and was living with her parents with little Jean, while baby Robert was with Burns's family. On a trip home to Mauchline, Jean and Robert 'reconciled' to the degree that Jean became pregnant once more. Jean's parents threw her out of the family home, but Burns returned home for good and found work as an exciseman. By the time their second pair of twins were born (Jean was good at twins), James Armour had agreed to their marriage on the basis of Burns's success as a poet.

Jean Armour and Robert Burns would have five more children together, the last of whom was born on the day of Burns's funeral in 1796. Robert's death left Jean almost destitute, and a charitable fund was established to support her and the children – including the daughter of Burns's mistress Anna Park. Jean survived her husband by thirty-eight years and despite having a clear sight of his personality – womanising, cheating and all – she cherished his memory fondly. For his part, he said that Jean had 'the handsomest figure, the sweetest temper, the soundest constitution, and the kindest heart in the county'.

LIVE YOUR LIFE BY JEAN

First off, be thankful for the fact we live in an era when contraception exists. Robert Burns has gone down in history as a bit of a shit thanks to the number of illegitimate children he fathered. Actually he slept with – what? Seven women we know of, maybe eight if 'Highland Mary' is included, and he tried it on with a few more. Hardly the world's most prolific shagger, but without access to contraception a brood of children resulted. Even within wedlock Burns and Jean might have been grateful for the chance to limit the size of their family. The sex, it seemed, was too good – at least if Burns's letters of enthusiastic exploits are to be believed.

Robert's praise for Jean demonstrates the way with words that got him into all those women's knickers, but others had kind words for her too. A visitor in the 1820s described a 55-year-old Jean as 'a very comely woman with plain sound sense and very good manners' and she was kindly regarded by many others for bringing up Anna Park's daughter Betty as her own. She even agreed to meet Agnes Maclehose in Edinburgh many years after Burns's death.

The greatest lesson from Jean's life? Be a signed-up, loyal member of the sisterhood; the alternative is to be a friend to the patriarchy.

MARY SOMERVILLE
MATHEMATICIAN AND POLYMATH

Mary Fairfax was born in Jedburgh in the Borders in 1780 and raised in Burntisland in Fife. Her parents were well connected but not wealthy and in order to make ends meet, her mother supplemented her father's naval salary by growing fruit and vegetables and keeping cows. Keen to ensure her daughter had the skills to make her own way in the world, Mary's mother taught her to read at home and then persuaded her father to send her to school for a year to learn to write and keep accounts.

At school Mary discovered a taste for learning that never left her. On returning home she began her own study of shells and sea-life and discovered fossils in the limestone that was shipped from the coast of Fife. She also started to work her way through the books in her father's library, alarming an elderly aunt who was concerned that her needlework might suffer – PASS THE SMELLING SALTS! As a result, Mary was sent to the local school to learn to sew; happily the schoolmaster got over it being the 18th century, recognised Mary's talents and taught her how to read the globes in her parents' home instead.

After a winter at school in Edinburgh when she was thirteen, Mary began to teach herself Latin in order to be able to read more of her father's books. She moved on to geometry and Greek and entered Alexander Nasmyth's Academy for Ladies in Edinburgh, where she became interested in astronomy and mechanical science. At home, Mary's studies had to take second place to more conventionally feminine pursuits such as music and painting. At least there

"From my earliest years my mind revolted against oppression and tyranny, and I resented the injustice of the world in denying all those privileges of education to my sex which were so lavishly bestowed on men."

MARY SOMERVILLE
REFLECTS ON HER EXPERIENCES IN *PERSONAL RECOLLECTIONS*

were benefits to these enforced social accomplishments – Mary began to build a circle of other enquiring minds, seeing her first laboratory and meeting many future scientists and thinkers.

Sadly, Mary's first husband, Samuel Greig, was not big on thinking, especially thinking done by women. When he died in 1807, after just three years of marriage, Mary took her inheritance, packed up her two children and returned home to Scotland where she resumed her studies. Maths was her particular interest, but she also studied astronomy, chemistry, geography, microscopy, electricity and magnetism. She made a happier choice of second husband in Dr William Somerville, who encouraged her in her studies and introduced her to a wider circle in the maths and science world. She had four further children of her own and tutored her friend's daughter, Ada Lovelace, in mathematics. Together with Mary, Ada viewed Charles Babbage's 'Difference Engine' – a calculating machine – and would go on to be credited as the first person in Britain to understand the potential of computers.

Mary published her first paper – on the magnetic properties of violet rays – in 1826 and went on to translate, edit, review and author books and papers on a huge range of subjects. She received a civil pension of £200 a year in recognition of her services to science and literature, and, in 1835, she jointly became the first woman member of the Royal Astronomical Society with Caroline Herschel. In 1842 she proposed the idea of a planet disrupting Uranus. John Couch Adams went hunting and discovered Neptune in 1846.

Books on geography and molecular and microscopic science followed, but Somerville's first love remained mathematics. She died in Naples aged ninety-one and her autobiography *Personal Recollections* was published the following year. The book reflects on her work and on her experiences in attempting to gain an education as a woman. Four years before her death, hers was the first signature on a petition for female suffrage. She was never to see it; she died thinking that 'British laws are adverse to women'.

Many memorials to Mary exist, from an Oxford College, to a crater on the moon, to a Scottish banknote issued in 2017. Perhaps the highest tribute is the word *scientist*, coined to replace 'man of science' in deference to Mary and her achievements.

LIVE YOUR LIFE BY MARY

Okay, rant coming up. There's a new term doing the rounds for women in science, and it's stupid. It's 'scientista'. Like . . . a *scientist* who is also a *lady*.

PLEASE, if you hear women using this term, point out to them that the term 'scientist' exists because of Mary Somerville. It's OURS. We don't need a separate term BECAUSE WE ARE CAPABLE OF THE SAME STUFF AS MEN. We're capable of medicine and we don't need to be called 'lady doctors', just 'doctors', and we can drive things and just be called 'drivers' or play football and be called 'footballers'.

Anything else is a step back that implies that it's men that actually have the right to do whatever it is we're discussing, and we're sort of pretending. Which is particularly stupid when it comes to being a 'scientist', a term that only exists because Mary Somerville proved that women are the equal of men in scientific thought, and indeed in thought in general. She banished the Man of Science label to the dustbin of history; let's not get it back out.

We can be anything we want to be, and we don't need special treatment and cute words, only equality of opportunity.

JAMES BARRY
DOCTOR

On 25 July 1865, the celebrated surgeon James Barry died. Barry had trained in Edinburgh and served the British Army from 1813, working in London and Plymouth before sailing to Cape Town in 1816. In Cape Town, Barry treated the daughter of the governor so successfully that he was immediately appointed as the governor's physician and later as Colonial Medical Inspector. In this role Barry improved sanitation and water systems, worked to improve conditions for slaves, prisoners and those suffering mental illness, and introduced provisions for the care of those with leprosy. He also performed a famous caesarean section in which both mother and child survived – a rare occurrence at the time. The child was named James Barry Munnik in the doctor's honour. Barry did not win over everyone so well – he was outspoken in his criticism of local officials' handling of medical care and sanitation, but his friendship with the governor protected him from repercussions.

Barry was promoted to Surgeon to the Forces in 1827 and worked in Mauritius, Jamaica and Saint Helena. He was then promoted to Principal Medical Officer in the Leeward and Windward Islands, where he again focused on introducing improvements in medical care, sanitation and troops' conditions. After a brief time recuperating from yellow fever in England, he was posted to Malta, where he dealt with a cholera epidemic, and Corfu, where he became Deputy Inspector-General of Hospitals.

"Was I not a girl I would be a Soldier!"

MARGARET ANN BULKLEY
WRITES TO HER BROTHER
1808

During this posting Barry visited the Crimea and fell out spectacularly with Florence Nightingale, who said that Barry was 'the most hardened creature I ever met throughout the army'. A posting in Canada followed, where Barry received the rank of Inspector General of Hospitals.

Barry had unusual ideas for the time, being vegetarian and teetotal, and limiting personal relationships to unavoidable social contact. He was devoted to his work, protesting greatly when age and ill health resulted in his being forcefully retired by the army in 1859. He travelled home to London and lived quietly, dying of dysentery in 1865. The woman who came to lay out the body stripped Barry and made a spectacular discovery. Barry was biologically female, and appeared to have borne a child.

The woman who had made the discovery attempted to use it to extract payment from Barry's friends, but when this was not forthcoming, she went to the press. A number of Barry's acquaintances proclaimed that they had suspected it might be the case all along. It was true that there had been some discussion of Barry's small size, high voice and smooth skin when he entered Edinburgh University's Medical School in 1809. It was assumed at the time that he was younger than he purported to be and the senate of the university briefly attempted to block his registration for final examinations on this basis. It seems only fair to note that the enthusiasm with which the university attempted to block Sophia Jex-Blake from matriculating in 1869 (see page 45) does render it unlikely that they overlooked the fact they had a woman on the roll sixty years earlier.

Barry's own physician speculated that Barry was an 'imperfectly developed man'. The woman who had viewed the body was scathing in her response to these propositions.

The British Army, ever an honourable institution, sealed Barry's records for one hundred years in the hope of hushing it all up. In the 1950s, historian Isobel Rae gained access to the records and her research, supplemented by that of Cape Town doctor Michael du Preez, revealed that Barry had been accompanied from Ireland to Edinburgh by his 'aunt' Mary Ann Bulkley, the sister of Irish artist and academic James Barry. Letters from the Bulkleys show that the younger 'James Barry' was in fact Mary Ann's daughter, Margaret Ann. James Barry senior had connections to radical politicians in Venezuela. With their support and that of a range of other connections, Margaret Ann Bulkley, who had railed against the binds of poverty and gender that prevented her from studying medicine or joining the army, had hatched a plan to study medicine in Edinburgh disguised as a man. The idea was then to travel to Venezuela where, once the radicals had taken charge, it would be possible to practise medicine as a woman.

When the planned liberation of Venezuela failed to materialise, 'Barry' instead hit on the idea of joining the army, which did not then require a medical examination at officer level. There may have been bumps in the road – Barry is said to have shot an officer in the lung for teasing him about his squeaky voice and there was gossip about a sexual relationship with the governor in Cape Town which introduces a tantalising element of *who knew?* to the story – but the audacious plan worked.

A sad footnote to Barry's story is the hypothesis that the child the laying-out woman considered Barry to have borne was possibly Barry's 'sister' Juliana Bulkley, and furthermore that she was conceived as the result of a sexual assault by a brother of Mary Ann Bulkley's.

·LIVE YOUR LIFE BY JAMES/MARGARET ANN

A recent novelisation of Barry's life attracted some controversy regarding the author's framing of Barry's gender identity. Opposing viewpoints emerged. At the furthest polarities, these held:

(1) that Barry was trans, anyone writing or discussing Barry should respect and adopt this interpretation, and to do otherwise is to deny the existence of trans people, in history and today;

(2) that Barry was a woman performing a charade, and claims otherwise are to deny the inequalities experienced by biological females throughout history, and potentially to perpetuate these today.

There are, of course, many interpretations on the spectrum between these two viewpoints.

Interpretation is the operative term here: we do not know how Barry thought about gender because we have no record at all of Barry's thoughts on the subject. We know of the plot that led to Margaret Ann Bulkley enrolling in Edinburgh University from surviving documentation. We know that Barry had, according to the lying-out woman, borne a child; again, this is documented. Many other aspects of Barry's life are documented too, but sources narrate the facts of events and the contemporary interpretations we assign are, again, speculation. We can speculate about other relationships from documented timelines, for example, and we may speculate as to what particular confidantes knew.

There is perhaps something in Barry's story about confidentiality, and privacy. Each of us is our own person and we don't owe an explanation of our inner self to anyone. While few of us face the sort of barriers Barry did to pursuing a chosen career – although gender remains a significant issue in the workplace today – many of us will choose to keep our personal and professional lives separate. That's part of the reason that low-grade sexism, discrimination and harassment in the workplace are such issues. Talent and determination should be what matters, and we should all be free to operate as professional beings without being reduced to objects by someone else. If such objectification happens to you, report it.

Recent controversies over Barry's story also remind us to be alive to our own perspectives and how these influence our analysis of others.

"Cuimhnichibh ur cruadal,
Is cumaibh suas ur sròl;
Gun tèid an roth mun cuairt duibh
Le neart is cruas nan dòrn . . ."

"Remember the hardship you have suffered
and keep your banners high
Until the wheel turns again for you
With fist-blows hard and strong . . ."

MARY MACPHERSON
ENCOURAGES CROFTERS IN 'EILEAN A' CHEÒ'
LATE 1800s

MÀIRI MHÒR NAN ÒRAN

MARY MACPHERSON

POET AND LAND CAMPAIGNER

The infamous Highland Clearances had begun in the 1700s and throughout the 1800s the relentless eviction of families from inland areas of Scotland to eke out a living on coastal fringes or cross the sea to Canada continued. But the tide was on the turn and by the mid-point of the century, violent resistance had become the order of the day. In the 1880s the crofters won a significant concession when Prime Minister Gladstone ordered a commission to gather evidence on the situation. Some part of this success was due to the efforts of one woman from Skye – Màiri Mhòr nan Òran, or Big Mary of the Songs.

Mary was born in 1821 and composed her poetry in the Gaelic tradition in which she was raised. Although she could read her own words written down by others, she was never able to write in her own language. Literacy in Gaelic was rare thanks to unenlightened educational policies – this remained the case until very recently – and Mary was therefore especially important as her songs spread word of the struggle across the Highlands.

Mary's poetry and political campaigning were inspired by an incident in 1871 which resulted in her being imprisoned for forty days, probably unjustly and for nonsense in any case. Her husband Isaac MacPherson had died and Mary had taken employment as a domestic servant with an army officer's family in Inverness. The wife of the officer died and Mary was accused of stealing some of her clothes. No records relating to the case survive, but Mary was traumatised by the experience and protested her innocence for the rest of her life. The trial brought her to the attention of John Murdoch of *The Highlander* newspaper, and of Charles Fraser-Mackintosh, solicitor and politician in Inverness. These friendships would last the rest of her life and Mary would contribute to both men's efforts in support of the crofters.

On her release from prison Mary moved to Glasgow, learned to read and write in English and qualified as a nurse and midwife at Glasgow Royal Infirmary. She became a mainstay of gatherings of Skye people in Glasgow, but her aim was always to go home and eventually she retired to Skye. She began to campaign actively in the Crofters' Wars, producing a raft of fine songs in support of the agitation, which she performed at political meetings and gatherings.

Mary's skills extended beyond poetry and oratory and into handwork. She designed Professor John Stuart Blackie his own tartan and spun and dyed the wool for a suit for Charles Fraser-Mackintosh. Fraser-Mackintosh was her friend to the last, paying to erect a gravestone to Mary and her husband in Chapel Yard Cemetery in Inverness upon her death in 1898. She is one of the few Gaelic-speaking women to have a blue plaque in her honour. It marks her last residence, the building that is now the Rosedale Hotel in Portree in Skye.

LIVE YOUR LIFE BY MARY

Scotland is a country with a rich linguistic heritage incorporating Gaelic, a Celtic language spoken here since around 200 AD; Scots, which derived from Anglo-Saxon and became common around 1400; and English, a late incursion which some reckon to have been a majority language in Scotland since only the 18th century. Along the way we've lost Pictish and other Celtic languages related to modern-day Welsh, Norman French, and others, and acquired a raft of modern languages including Urdu, Hindi, Italian, Polish and dozens more.

For some reason, it's fashionable in Scotland to moan about all languages except English. Scots is dismissed as 'bad English' or 'slang', as though several million people speak the way they speak on a daily basis just to be difficult and they should all start impersonating the Queen or people in Albert Square instead. Gaelic comes into the firing line for reasons as random as the fact it doesn't have a word for 'helicopter'. It doesn't – it was actively supressed for generations and didn't have the chance to develop in new contexts – but then again, English doesn't have it own one either and instead borrowed one from Greek via French in the 19th century. Occasionally this all reaches peak stupidity as English-only speakers complain that Gaelic doesn't have its own word for 'car', which is actually a Celtic term borrowed into English. So stick that up your exhaust pipe, or *pìob-thraoghaidh* if you prefer.

Remember Mary, who was denied education in her native language and learned to read and write in an entirely different one later in life. You don't have to learn Gaelic, or any other language if you don't want to, but channel Mary any time you think of criticising of other people for using their own language and *just don't be a dick about it.*

"The reason he did not make me his Wife was because he was disgusted with my person the first evening."

EFFIE GRAY
WRITES TO HER FATHER
1853

EFFIE GRAY
MANAGER, MODEL AND MUSE

Euphemia Chalmers Gray was born in Perth in May 1828. From childhood she had known John Ruskin, the eminent art critic. The Ruskin family was also from Perth, and when John's father moved to London to develop his wine business, the Grays moved into their family home. Little 'Phemy', as she was then known, stayed with the Ruskins during school holidays and John wrote a fairy tale for her, *The King of the Golden River*, when she was twelve years old.

John was ten years Effie's senior, an only child doted on by his parents and raised in a household dominated by his mother's poor health and intense religious belief. By the age of twelve, the poor sod was making his own fun, and that fun was in the shape of 2,000-plus line poems inspired by family travels. He was useless with the opposite sex – in fact, he was shy of strangers in general. 'If I had been a woman,' he wrote of himself, 'I never should have loved the kind of person that I am.' In fairness, much that subsequently happened does make him seem pretty unattractive to the modern eye, so maybe he had that self-assessment spot on.

Effie, on the other hand, was a lively, flirtatious character with a parade of admirers. Ruskin declared his affection for her in a series of distinctly uncomfortable letters. 'Merciless' and 'mischief-loving', he called her, 'saucy', 'torturing' and 'wicked'. Initially his affections were not returned but in 1848 a match was arranged between the families and the two were married. Effie was nineteen, and John twenty-nine.

The newlyweds travelled to Venice, where the difference in their personalities immediately became apparent. John's idea of a honeymoon involved drawing the Doge's Palace and other architectural gems he feared would be destroyed by occupying Austrian troops, with the aim of completing his new book. Effie was very much left to her own devices, and revelled in Venice society.

In 1852, Effie began to model for the painter John Everett Millais. The following year John invited Millais to travel to Scotland with the Ruskins to paint his portrait. On what must have been a spectacularly uncomfortable trip, Millais and Effie fell in love. On their return to London, Effie announced that she was leaving to visit family. She never returned to Ruskin. From her family home she returned her wedding ring with a note: she planned to file for annulment on the grounds that her marriage had never been consummated. Almost six years later, she was still a virgin.

The revelations caused a scandal. 'He alleged various reasons, hatred to children, religious motives, a desire to preserve my beauty, and, finally this last year he told me his true reason . . . that he had imagined women were quite different to what he saw I was,' Effie wrote to her father. John in turn confirmed this state of affairs in a statement to his lawyer. '[T]hough her face was beautiful,' he said, 'her person was not formed to excite passion. On the contrary, there were certain circumstances in her person which completely checked it.' The meaning of this nastiness has been endlessly discussed – common theories range from revulsion at her pubic hair to horror at menstrual blood or dislike of her body odour. Supporters of Ruskin suggest that he was actually horrified by her family's financial motivations for arranging the marriage, too proud to sleep with her under these circumstances and therefore should be seen as a general all-round good guy for agreeing to pretend the problem was an issue with intimacy on his part.

In 1854 the marriage was annulled on grounds of 'incurable impotency'. Effie was free to marry Millais. She made up for her sterile marriage to Ruskin in style with eight children and was an effective partner in managing Millais's career, modelling for him on several occasions. In full-on shade-throwing bitch mode, John called his later painting style 'a catastrophe'.

And what of those suggestions that John was just a poor dupe taken in by a fortune hunter? Aside from the fact that it requires that we put aside what Effie wrote and what Ruskin swore, Ruskin later sought to marry another teenage girl,

Rose de la Touche. They had met when she was nine and he was thirty-eight. After correspondence with Effie, Rose's parents refused their permission. When she came of age, Rose agreed to marry Ruskin on the condition the marriage remained unconsummated. He refused.

LIVE YOUR LIFE BY EFFIE

Bad as some modern gender politics may be, we now recognise the concept of grooming, and John's courting of a much younger girl he had known since her childhood would not – one fervently hopes – be accepted today. Our reality is still far from perfect – too many of us will recognise the bullying in John's behaviour because we have also experienced the exercise of male power in the bedroom in ways that have disturbed or demeaned us.

Effie has something to teach us, too, in her frankness in discussing the ways in which John bullied and belittled her. By naming and shaming, she regained considerable power – indeed, she regained control of her life. One way we might benefit from her example is to learn to discuss our bodies without shame or negativity – even to name our intimate parts. If we can't do it, how can we communicate our needs, our health issues and even our preferences for pleasure? It's most certainly a power worth cultivating.

Lastly: three cheers for Effie's father, whose strong and respectful relationship with his daughter is evident from her frankness in writing to him of the distressing realities of her marriage, and a round of boos for those in the modern era who would still defend John and his behaviour.

"It is a grand thing to enter the very first British University ever opened to women, isn't it?"

SOPHIA JEX~BLAKE
WRITES TO HER FRIEND LUCY SEWELL IN BOSTON
1869

'THE EDINBURGH SEVEN'

SOPHIA JEX-BLAKE
ISABEL THORNE
EDITH PECHEY
MATILDA CHAPLIN
HELEN EVANS
MARY ANDERSON
AND EMILY BOVELL

SEEKERS AFTER LEARNING

Edinburgh University's Faculty of Medicine has a proud history. Established in 1726, it is the oldest medical school in the United Kingdom, and, until well into the 20th century, it was widely considered the best in the English-speaking world. When Sophia Jex-Blake applied to study there in 1869 it had been home to many important developments in the medical field, including the introduction of chloroform and of antiseptics. It had also seen its fair share of scandal, buying cadavers from grave robbers and even from murderers in the forms of Burke and Hare. But, hey, the faculty and many of its students could apparently reconcile themselves with suspicious bruising on the necks of their anatomy specimens. What they could not accept was the idea of a WOMAN studying in their midst.*

to their knowledge (see page 31)

Sophia Jex-Blake was born in Hastings in 1840, studied in London and travelled to America to work with Lucy Sewell in the New England Hospital for Women and Children in Boston. In 1867 she sought to be admitted to Harvard University's medical programme. The New World proved itself just as prejudiced as the Old; Harvard, the reply read, could offer 'no provision for the education of women in any department of this university'.

In 1868, Sophia's father died and she returned to England to support her mother. She was still preoccupied with the radical idea that women could compete with men if only they were offered 'a fair field and no favour', and continued to seek a place at medical school. She decided that her best chance lay in Scotland, where attitudes to education were perhaps not quite so unenlightened as they were elsewhere, and she applied to Edinburgh. Despite a petition against her signed by over two hundred students, the Medical Faculty and Academic Senate approved her application. The university court then rejected it on the basis that the university could not make the necessary arrangements 'in the interest of one lady'.

Sophia decided to take them at the word and arranged for articles in *The Scotsman* imploring other women to join her. That summer a further five 'ladies' applied for the right to matriculate as students (thankfully there was no below-the-line commenting in *The Scotsman* in those days or chances are they'd have given up in despair). By the time the case was heard by the university court, the group had grown to seven.

The application was approved, the women studied for the matriculation exam and four of them ranked among the top seven students to sit it. On 2 November 1869 they signed the matriculation roll, meaning that Edinburgh had become the first university in Britain to open its doors to women despite the best efforts of its student body. Sophia wrote to Lucy Sewell in Boston to express her delight. Her joy was short-lived.

The women were taught separately from male students and paid higher fees as their classes were smaller. Otherwise, they were treated exactly as the men were, and accordingly, they sat their first exams in March 1870. All passed, with Edith Pechey winning first place. This entitled her to a prestigious Hope Scholarship, but NATURALLY she was passed over for a man with lower marks, her professor fearing the fallout should the award be given to a woman.

In April, the university court held a debate to decide on whether the women should be allowed in mixed classes, meaning that they would be eligible for prizes and their elevated fees would be reduced. Two professors accused the women of loose morals in the crudest of terms. The national press took up the women's case – the national press weirdly sounds better in this story than it is today on the feminism front – but at the same time many staff who had agreed to teach them began to turn away. The Seven endured abuse at the hands of the male students, who vandalised their rooms, wrote to them in obscene terms and shouted 'whore' at them in the street.

On Friday 18 November 1870, the abuse culminated in a riot when the women arrived to sit an anatomy exam. Male students pelted them with mud and rubbish and insulted them in the street. The main gates of the building were slammed in their faces. When they were eventually admitted, the exam was disrupted as protesters released a live sheep into the hall.

The Surgeon's Hall Riot, as it came to be known, marked a turning point in attitudes towards the women, with new supporters across society including Charles Darwin, who joined a General Committee for Securing a Complete Medical Education for Women. But in 1873 the Court of Session supported the University's right to refuse the women degrees. The Court ruled that the women should not have been admitted in the first place.

The Seven paved the way for women to enter higher education in Scotland, but the right to graduate would not be granted until the Universities (Scotland) Act of 1889. Five of the Seven travelled overseas to obtain their degrees, and four first secured their license to practise in Ireland. Edith Pechey practised as a doctor in Leeds and then India. She was appointed to the senate of the University of Bombay. Matilda Chaplin founded a midwifery school in Tokyo and later practised privately in London. Emily Bovell and Mary Anderson worked at the New Hospital for Women in London, Isabel Thorne became honorary secretary of the London School of Medicine for Women, and Helen Evans joined the executive committee of the Edinburgh School of Medicine for Women.

Sophia Jex-Blake returned to Edinburgh, became the city's first female doctor, and helped found the Edinburgh School of Medicine for Women. After her death her partner Dr Margaret Todd – who helped coin the term *isotope* – wrote a book of her life.

The University of Edinburgh first allowed women to graduate in 1894 and the first doctors graduated in 1896. They still had to organise their own tuition.

As for Harvard? The first women accepted there did not enter the Medical School until 1936.

LIVE YOUR LIFE BY THE SEVEN

Sophia Jex-Blake could not have achieved what she did without the support and encouragement of the rest of the Seven and of many others in the university and in society. From the *Scotsman* editor who ran her appeal to the women who answered, and the male students who stood up to their peers to escort the Seven to and from classes to the professors who taught them, their story is full of those who wished to help and saw the unfairness of their situation. They reached out, made connections and took action, and while they were frustrated for many years by structures beyond their control, their actions saw results in the end.

Tempting as it is to think that social media today is the equivalent of Sophia's *Scotsman* appeal, too often it is a discussion in an echo-chamber, and very much too often we use it not to help drive progress or for acts of kindness but rather to moan, time-waste, make ourselves feel good with zero effort – click to share – or, worst of all, we take part in personal attacks or otherwise make other people feel bad. And over-use of social media can result in a fear of missing out (FOMO) that keeps us in the virtual world when, actually, we're missing out in reality.

Step away from the screen now and then and get involved in something you care about in the real world. Helping does take time and effort, but the payback is that you are actually helping. And when you are online, get used to thinking twice before you post or share.

WILLIAMINA FLEMING
ASTRONOMER

illiamina Stevens fell into the trap that has caught many good women throughout history – she married a rotten man. Perhaps the 1800s weren't bursting with men ready to embrace a woman with Williamina's intellect, but even by the standards of the time James Orr Fleming was a shit. He married his 22-year-old bride, sailed with her to America and abandoned her in Boston, pregnant and destitute. Williamina found work as a maid to support herself and her child. Good fortune took her to the home of Edward Charles Pickering, the director of the Harvard College Observatory.

Pickering's wife soon noticed that Williamina's talents reached beyond the domestic sphere and Pickering himself was evidently impressed by her intellect. The story goes that he regularly became frustrated by the performance of the male data processors at the Observatory, loudly complaining, 'My Scottish maid could do better!'

When one of Pickering's processors – known as 'computers' – left the Observatory, he offered Williamina work as her replacement. She rose to manage a team of women computers inspecting and analysing spectral images. With Pickering, she developed a classification scheme to distill stellar spectra into categories and personally created the most extensive star compilation of the era. She lamented the onerous nature of her work as the observatory's production and publication supervisor as it limited her time for original work, but her accomplishments were still prodigious.

"I am immediately told that I receive an excellent salary as women's salaries stand . . . Does he ever think that I have a home to keep and a family to take care of as well as the men? . . . And this is considered an enlightened age!"

WILLIAMINA FLEMING
CONFRONTS CHARLES EDWARD PICKERING OVER
SALARY DISCREPANCIES BETWEEN MEN AND WOMEN
LATE 1800s

Williamina discovered 10 novae, 59 gaseous nebulae and more than 300 variable stars in her career. She identified Orion's Horsehead Nebula and became the first American woman to be honoured by the Royal Astronomical Society.

'If one could only go on and on with original work,' she wrote, '. . . life would be a most beautiful dream.'

LIVE YOUR LIFE BY WILLIAMINA

When you next want to negotiate a pay rise or indeed a starting salary in a new job, think of Williamina. Women are still paid less than men; the gender pay gap in the UK fell in 2018 after a huge awareness-raising campaign saw many employers vow to tackle the issue, but it still stood at 8.6 per cent at the year-end. Some campaigners point out this means that women effectively aren't paid for more than one month in the year, while men in equivalent roles continue to draw their salaries. Part of the reason for the gap may be that women are not encouraged to value themselves as openly as men do.

On that note, the next time you pick up a piece of pink plastic or a contouring kit for your niece, your daughter or your little sister's birthday, think of Williamina. Could you buy a science kit, a really inspiring book or an age-appropriate equivalent such as a planting kit instead, and help create a genius of the future? Women make up well under 20 per cent of the UK's STEM workforce; there's plenty of opportunity for little Williaminas to make their mark on the world.

"If the English Government will not have us, let us offer ourselves to other Allied Governments; the need is pressing everywhere."

ELSIE INGLIS
REFUSES TO TAKE NO FOR AN ANSWER
1914

ELSIE INGLIS
DOCTOR AND SUFFRAGIST

With the words opposite, Dr Elsie Inglis introduced colleagues to the idea that became the Scottish Women's Hospitals, vital medical facilities on the fronts of the First World War. She offered her services first to the War Office, and despite her considerable reputation, was told, as she put it; 'My good lady, go home and sit still.'

Elsie was not one to be told to 'sit still' by some old duffer; she was already a medical and social pioneer. Born in 1864 in Naini Tal, India, to enlightened parents who considered education no less important for a daughter than a son, she attended school in Edinburgh and Paris and determined to study medicine despite the small obstacle that women were not accepted onto most medical courses of the era. In 1887 she entered Dr Sophia Jex-Blake's Edinburgh School of Medicine for Women. Jex-Blake might have been a pioneer for her campaign to enter Edinburgh University (see page 45); sadly it seems that she was no great shakes as a teacher. Elsie left and founded her own breakaway medical college, The Edinburgh College of Medicine for Women. She completed her own training at Glasgow Royal Infirmary, qualifying as a member of the Royal College of Physicians of Edinburgh, the Royal College of Surgeons of Edinburgh and the Faculty of Physicians and Surgeons of Glasgow. When at last Edinburgh University opened its medical school properly to women, she graduated as Bachelor of Medicine, Bachelor of Surgery.

From the earliest days of her training, Elsie was appalled at the poor standards of care for female patients, an area in which few doctors specialised at the time. She joined Elizabeth Garrett Anderson's New Hospital for Women in London and then the Rotunda maternity hospital in Dublin. Inspired by these examples, she returned to Edinburgh in 1894 to set up medical practice with a female colleague and founded a maternity hospital, the Hospice, at 219 High Street (now, naturally, replaced with a tourist tat shop).

Elsie's interest in medical care for women was deeply political at a time when a husband could refuse medical treatment on his wife's behalf. Seeing that change was necessary at every level, Elsie became involved with the campaign for votes for women. She was not a suffrag*ette* undertaking militant action; rather she was a suffrag*ist*, working with Millicent Fawcett in England to help suffrage societies pool their resources. Through Elsie, the Federation of Women's Suffrage Societies launched the Scottish Women's Hospitals for Foreign Service. The aim was to open relief hospitals staffed exclusively by women to support the Allied war effort – and to draw men's attention to women's capabilities. 'So much of our work is done where they cannot see it,' Elsie said. 'They'll see every bit of this.' The first funds for the service came from her own pocket.

Denied support by the War Office and the Scottish Red Cross, Elsie approached the French government and the first Scottish Women's Hospital was established in France. The network grew to cover fronts as far afield as Serbia and Romania. She was herself taken prisoner in Serbia and was forcibly returned home but immediately began raising funds for a Russian team she headed up herself.

Elsie died of cancer in Edinburgh in 1917. Among the many memorials to her was Edinburgh's Elsie Inglis Memorial Hospital, established in 1925, primarily as a maternity hospital, and the birthplace of many of the capital's children in the 20th century.

LIVE YOUR LIFE BY ELSIE

The attitudes Elsie faced are still around, and perhaps all the more dangerous since the narrative that we pretty much have equality is gaining some traction despite the fact that a majority of UK companies still pay women less than men, one in five UK women will be a victim of sexual assault, and a razor marketed at women typically costs 37 per cent more than one marketed at men. Oh, and a self-declared woman-assaulter holds the US presidency.

'Feminism' is another way of saying 'equality for women'. It does not mean a person is 'anti-men' and anyone who tells you it does is taking part in a monstering designed to ensure that women can't have equality, ever. Anyone who tells you that it is exclusive of other groups suffering inequality is also wrong; rather depressingly people can suffer discrimination because of their biological gender AND ethnicity, sexuality or other characteristics and we need to tackle all of these, not prevent the tackling of any one in particular. You've heard of the concept of divide and rule? Shoving down efforts to eliminate discrimination for one group ostensibly to promote equality for another is a perfect example of how that works. The end result is no one gets equality, and those who are doing nicely out of inequality get to continue on their merry way, thank you very much.

So go on, embrace feminism. We should all be equal, and feminism is an international movement to ensure that women aren't denied equality for the specific reason that they are women. You might like to start with *Dear Ijeawele* by Chimamanda Ngozi Adichie; it's marvellous.

"She is about the most courageous woman I ever saw. She seems to be without fear or nerves, is very good at her job and has an uncanny power over engines."

FIRST MATE WARNER, *BONITA*, ON VICTORIA DRUMMOND

VICTORIA DRUMMOND
MARINE ENGINEER

When Victoria Drummond visited the engineering works of Robert Morton and Sons in Errol, Perthshire, in the 1910s, she asked Mr Morton a surprising question. How could she become a marine engineer? Did Mr Morton laugh at this privileged young lady's curiosity? No, he did not. He told her the answer: first she should serve an apprenticeship, and then find a shop with a vacancy. Once she had served her time, she would need to find a berth as an engineer. Three cheers for Mr Morton, a good feminist, even if he wouldn't have recognised the term.

Before she could embark on this path, Victoria had more obvious business to discharge for a young lady of her class. This was the era of the débutante, when young ladies 'came of age' by being paraded in front of the King and/or Queen in a white dress. Victoria took part in this lovely ritual but two years later, she turned twenty-one, and she immediately swapped her frock for a set of overalls.

From October 1916, Victoria was apprenticed at the Northern Garage in Perth, earning half a crown a week. Three evenings a week were spent studying maths and engineering. She then moved to the Caledon Shipbuilding and Engineering Company in Dundee, where she completed her apprenticeship in 1920.

In 1922 Victoria wrote to the Blue Funnel Line to seek a place as an engineer. Her first voyage was on the passenger liner *Anchises* from Liverpool to

Glasgow. She passed this trial and was taken on as Tenth Engineer, serving on four voyages to Australia and one to China. In the main the passengers and crew accepted having a woman engineer, but idiots turn up everywhere and a few passed derogatory remarks. This would be theme of the rest of her peacetime service, during which she qualified as a Second Engineer. There her career stalled. Despite repeatedly sitting the examination for Chief Engineer, she failed again and again. Privately, the examiners admitted that they failed her because she was a woman. See? Idiots everywhere.

After some years ashore, Victoria applied to return to sea in 1939, seeing that war was inevitable. Despite her previous service, every one of her applications was denied. Finally she enlisted as an air-raid warden in London, continuing to visit the docks in the hope of finding a ship to take her on. After exhausting British options, she signed with a Palestinian ship, *Har Zion*. Again she struggled with negative attitudes towards her, eventually leaving the ship as a result. It was a lucky escape; *Har Zion* was sunk by a German U-boat in 1940.

Victoria next joined *Bonita*, a ship from Panama. In August 1940, *Bonita* was in the North Atlantic when the Luftwaffe attacked. Despite losing the use of one eye in the attack, Drummond took the ship to 12.5 knots – 3 knots faster than her previous record – and the captain changed course, eluding the attackers.

For her service aboard *Bonita*, Victoria was awarded an MBE and the Lloyd's War Medal for Bravery at Sea. She was also awarded the Chief Engineer qualification she had always sought – by Panama. At home, the Board of Trade had now refused her on thirty-one occasions, and continued to do so.

Victoria served for the remainder of the war, including a stint shuttling supplies for the Invasion of Normandy. After the war she continued her career at sea, making forty-nine ocean-going voyages in forty years.

LIVE YOUR LIFE BY VICTORIA

In her early years, Victoria fell in with her parents' expectations, but she never forgot to be her own person. Her mother was the more conservative of the Drummonds – her dad believed in Victoria's right to choose her own career – but in the end she managed to balance the white frock and the presentation at court with what she really wanted for herself.

Life is much easier with the 'rents onside, so keep yourself in their good books if you can, and listen to what they say – they do want the best for you. That doesn't mean you have to do what they want if it really, really means you can't be true to yourself, but learning to be a grown-up involves listening to other opinions, and being willing to consider the options.

"Fancy [. . .] lolling about doing nothing when there is such a tremendous lot to do here. It's too rotten to think of."

MAIRI CHISHOLM
WRITES TO HER AUNT FROM BELGIUM
1914

MAIRI CHISHOLM

MOTOR-RACER AND MEDIC

Many little brothers and sisters are inspired to action by their older siblings; the impressively monickered Mairi Lambert Gooden-Chisholm of Chisholm was no exception. Her older brother Uailean's life seemed one of great excitement as he travelled the country on his Royal Enfield 425cc motorcycle, competing in rallies and speed trials. Her mother was horrified at Mairi's determination to get involved in the action – upper class Scottish daughters were not generally encouraged to take up motorcycling – but her father was on side. He bought her a Douglas motorbike of her own and she spent hours stripping it down and repairing it to roar around the lanes of Hampshire and Dorset, where the family had settled. On one of these excursions she met fellow motorcyclist Elsie Knocker, and the two became firm friends, competing together in motorcycle and sidecar trials.

When war was declared in 1914, Elsie was thirty-one and Mairi was just eighteen. Elsie proposed that they should both take their bikes to London where they could become dispatch riders for the Women's Emergency Corps. They duly signed up and were soon taking corners at speed all across the capital, carrying paperwork and other urgent deliveries. On one death-defying ride Mairi was spotted by Dr Hector Munro, then setting up the Flying Ambulance Corps, an unofficial ambulance service at the Front. Impressed by Mairi's abilities with her bike, Munro asked her to join. 'He said, "Would you like to go out to Flanders?" Mairi later recalled. 'And I said "Yes, I'd love to."' She was still just eighteen.

In Belgium, the women were based first in Ghent and then Furnes, where they picked up wounded soldiers behind the front lines and transported them to field hospitals at the rear. This was grim work, with rows upon rows of corpses and men with terrible injuries.

Despite all they had done so far, Mairi and Elsie wanted to do more. They were convinced more lives could be saved were soldiers treated directly on the front lines. They left the Flying Ambulance Corps and set up their own dressing station in a reinforced cellar in the town of Pervyse (Pervijze), north of Ypres. Here they were just yards from the trenches; Elsie could give emergency treatment to the wounded, and then Mairi would ferry them to a base hospital in a Wolsely ambulance, often under heavy fire. Initially funding their own work, the women eventually managed to become officially attached to the Belgian garrison in the town. King Albert I of Belgium awarded them the Order of Leopold II and they received the British Military Medal for saving a wounded pilot from No Man's Land. They became celebrities, known in the press as 'The Madonnas of Pervyse'.

During the three and a half years they were based in Pervyse, Mairi and Elsie survived heavy bombardment, sniper fire and gas attacks. Mairi contracted septicaemia and her health never fully recovered. She became engaged to pilot Jack Petrie, who died a year later on a practice run. Mairi and Elsie survived a massive bombing raid and gas attacks in 1918 and Mairi managed to return to their base once she had recuperated, but she was forced to abandon her post again before the end of the war. Back in Britain, she and Elsie joined the new Women's Royal Air Force and served until the Armistice.

Mairi and Elsie's fame clung on after the war, but their friendship did not survive. Despite lingering ill effects on her health, Mairi continued to live life in the fast lane for a time, giving up motorcycles and instead taking up auto racing. On her doctors' advice, she moved home to Scotland where she became a successful poultry farmer and took up an interest in clan genealogy, living with her childhood friend May Davidson for almost sixty years until her death in 1981.

LIVE YOUR LIFE BY MAIRI

Be a good mate, pick good mates, and your bezzie friendships can be some of the most significant relationships of your life. The details of why Mairi and Elsie's friendship foundered involve a social convention that seems stupid now – Elsie lied about being a widow when she was really a divorcée – but the real issue was trust, and Elsie didn't trust Mairi enough to tell her the truth.

True friends are the ones who you are happy to let see you warts-and-all, whether you're sobbing your mascara off over a break-up or puking your guts out after a leetle too much vodka. Follow the BFF honour code of being there for them, and they'll be there for you, for the rest of your life.

"Having imagined beforehand,
very precisely and very gently,
The white cot by my bed,
the old cot with the new green blankets,
The new dark soft head,
the faint breathing,
the warmth and love,
the ghost of the cot is still
there when I turn to my right,
And when I turn to my left,
there is the sea, there is Carradale Bay,
and sea-deep,
Dark and alone where the Cluaran
dropped her, my dear, my daughter,
Not in my arms, not in my womb: in the
box Angus made, a small weight."

FROM 'CLEMENCY EALASAID' BY
NAOMI MITCHISON
JULY 1940

NAOMI MITCHISON
WRITER

Naomi Haldane came from determined people. Her father was famous for subjecting himself and his children to potentially dangerous experiments designed to further understanding of the human body and its response to gases. Among his inventions was the 'Black Veil', an early respirator used to combat the effects of gas in First World War. The Haldane women were equally strong; Naomi's aunt Elizabeth was Scotland's first female Justice of the Peace and her mother a fierce feminist.

Naomi was born in Edinburgh in 1897 and initially planned to follow the family path into science, studying genetics with her brother. The outbreak of war in 1914 interrupted this plan, and Naomi trained as a nurse and then married a young barrister, Dick Mitchison. Dick was on leave from the Western Front at the time; after the war he became a Queen's Counsel and subsequently a Labour MP. Naomi was active in supporting her husband's political career but there were depths to which she would not stoop; when Dick received a life peerage in 1964, she flat-out refused to call herself Lady Mitchison.

After the early years of their marriage, Naomi and Dick agreed that theirs should become an open relationship and both entered into a number of other liaisons. Naomi had strongly expressed feminist beliefs and advocated for the ready availability of birth control. She openly discussed her own lack of knowledge of the subject, and its importance to her given that she wished to ensure that her children were conceived with her husband. She wrote that she dreamed of a future in which her daughters could create families in whatever image they chose.

Naomi lost two of her seven children. Geoffrey died of meningitis in 1927 at age nine. Clemency Ealasaid was born with a heart defect in 1940 and did not survive. Naomi wrote on these losses, and more generally on female strength and power, women's influence and their acts of sacrifice. She was no stranger to discrimination in both her literary and political activities; she found herself side-lined as a woman in male-dominated spheres.

In the late 1930s, Naomi and Dick bought Carradale House in Kintyre, and lived there for the rest of their lives. Carradale was a house full of visitors, with lords and ladies, politicians, writers, farmers and fisherman all in residence at various times. In the middle of this maelstrom sat Naomi at her typewriter, generating her enormous output. The story goes that she wrote so many books, she lost count.

Naomi's writing spans a huge range of styles and genres, from historical fiction to children's non-fiction, works on sexuality and on ethics, travel writing, poetry, memoir, science fiction and fantasy. She was also a prolific letter-writer, an essayist and journalist, a practical farmer and a botanist, and she was heavily involved in development activity in Argyll and the Highlands more generally, and in Botswana. A generous critic and correspondent, she supported her friend J.R.R. Tolkein on the not-inconsiderable task of checking the manuscript of *Lord of the Rings*, a book rivalled by her own *The Corn King and the Spring Queen* in its epic scale and synthesis of folklore, myth and history. PLUS IT HAS WOMEN IN IT.

Naomi was still writing, campaigning and being generally impressive well into her nineties. Indeed, on her ninetieth birthday she was asked about her regrets in life and her answer was that she regretted all the men she hadn't slept with. She died in Carradale at the age of one hundred and one.

LIVE YOUR LIFE BY NAOMI

As long ago as 1935, Naomi was subject to censorship for her book *We Have Been Warned* and its frank treatment of sex, rape and abortion. Nearly a hundred years later, women's bodies, experiences of sex and general 'issues' are still treated in much of society as something to be spoken of in hushed voices, if at all. We struggle to say 'vagina', let alone 'vulva', we don't tell anyone we're pregnant 'until it's safe', we don't discuss miscarriage or abortion, we don't like to mention things like ovarian cancer or endometriosis. And we certainly don't tell colleagues that we're having a rotten time with our period, even though it's difficult to imagine the males in our lives standing there in agony losing significant amounts of blood and *just not mentioning it*, isn't it?

Follow Naomi's lead and name it. Say it. Be shameless. Why on earth should we cringe at our bodily functions and the names of our body parts? 'Actually, I'm feeling a bit ropey this week for perfectly natural reasons relating to my uterus. Could you help me out?' Or, 'Could you please pick up some tampons for me at the supermarket? Ta.' It's quite empowering.

If you need to speak to a teacher, to your boss, or to your colleagues if you are the boss, ask to do so in private if you feel more comfortable, or ask for HR or your guidance teacher. If you're not quite badass enough yet, try downloading the information you need to communicate and hand it over.

If you have the resources, you could also consider donating toiletries and sanitary products to food banks for women and girls in need.

"There is not much
to report from here.
Even here on the
way to Heaven are
mountains,
but further away
than ours."

JANE HAINING
WRITES FROM AUSCHWITZ~BIRKENAU
1944

JANE HAINING

MATRON OF THE SCOTTISH MISSION SCHOOL, BUDAPEST

I n 2017 Zoltan Toth-Heinemann travelled from Hungary to the small Scottish village of Dunscore, eight miles from Dumfries. He was there to visit the place where Jane Haining worshipped, for inspiration for an exhibition in the Budapest Holocaust Memorial Centre.

Jane was born in Dunscore in 1897 and grew up on her father's farm. The family attended church in Dunscore, and Jane became a fervent evangelist. After some years working in Glasgow, she volunteered for missionary service in 1932 and travelled to Hungary where the Church of Scotland was active in running a Mission School for around four hundred mainly Jewish children. Jane became Matron, and was popular among pupils and colleagues alike. One former pupil remembered her as giving, 'all the love that she could'.

In 1939, the Second World War broke out. Jane, home on leave, was on holiday in Cornwall when she heard the news. Immediately she returned to Budapest. Hungary had traded with Italy and Germany throughout the 1930s as it sought to save its economy from recession. In 1940, under pressure from Germany, it joined the Axis powers. The Church of Scotland instructed its missionaries to return home for their own safety. Jane wrote back, 'If these children need me in days of sunshine, how much more do they need me in days of darkness?'

Jane lived with her girls in Budapest until 1944, when Hungary sought an armistice with the United States and the United Kingdom. German forces invaded. Jewish citizens had been protected from deportation during the early war years, despite widespread discrimination against them in Hungarian society. Now the deportations began. Again Jane was asked to leave; again she refused.

In April 1944 two Gestapo men arrived at the Mission, searched Jane's office and told her to gather her things. Still she sought to protect her pupils from any distress, telling them, 'Don't worry, I'll be back by lunch.' Charges against her included working among Jews, aiding prisoners of war and listening to the BBC. She admitted all charges but political activity. Attempts were made to secure her release, as letters by Bishop László Ravasz of the Reformed Church in Hungary found later showed. All attempts failed; she was transferred to Auschwitz via a holding camp on 15 May 1944. She was tattooed as prisoner 79467.

Jane's last communication was a postcard to her friend Margit Prem on 15 July 1944, asking for food. It ended with the words, 'There is not much to report from here. Even here on the way to Heaven are mountains, but further away than ours.' Starved and weak, Jane died in the Auschwitz hospital block on 16 August 1944, aged forty-seven.

In 2017, Zoltan Toth-Heinmann's exhibition about Jane opened in the Holocaust Memorial Centre in Budapest, followed by a permanent exhibition in Dunscore Church. She is the only Scot recorded as Righteous Among the Nations at Yad Vashem, the World Holocaust Remembrance Centre in Jerusalem.

LIVE YOUR LIFE BY JANE

Jane was an extraordinary woman who made admirable decisions based on her strong personal beliefs and the extraordinary – and terrible – circumstances she found herself in. Pay tribute by taking the chances we have in the modern day to explore the world. Don't just be a tourist – follow Jane's example and learn another language. Jane became fluent in both Hungarian and German; she knew the great pleasure other languages can give, the different windows on the world, the close friendships with speakers of those languages.

Jane's last card is quoted here in English, but it was written in German, the language of her friendship with Margit Prem. If you are a Westerner, you will find people from Ethiopia to Ecuador who are pleased to speak with a person who has taken the trouble to learn some – or a lot – of their language. You will suddenly find that you feel more at home in the world, a whole host of poems and songs have opened up to you, and you will hear stories you could not have imagined.

"I'll be glad to get sat
doon and have a nice
cup of tea."

MAW BROON

MAW BROON

MATRIARCH

Maw Broon is a woman so trauchled she hasn't managed to pick names for her last three bairns, and is it any wonder?

Maw has lived at Number 10 Glebe Street, Auchenshoogle, since 1936, with her husband Paw, sons Hen, Joe, Horace and the Twins, and daughters Maggie, Daphne and the Bairn. Think about it – this is a woman sharing a two-bedroom flat with eight children and no labour-saving appliances more modern than a mangle. If her own home and her enormous brood weren't enough to keep anyone busy, she is also a semi-carer for Paw's delinquent father, Granpaw Broon. When Granpaw's not spreading rumours, falling oot with his cronies, or breaking his false teeth on a granny sooker, he's up to some other mischief. Like that time he hooked out Maw's newly planted bulbs from under the bed and wired into the mixture in the mistaken impression he'd found some potted heid.

On occasion Maw makes it away from the family for long enough to take in a picture with a bag of jube-jubes, and there's always the family trips to the But 'n Ben to look forward to. But when she's busy black-leading the stove or cooking mince and tatties for eleven, it's tempting to wonder just how hard Maw wishes one of those adult bairns of hers would finally up and find a wee place of their own.

For many years Maw's given name was shrouded in mystery, as was her background, although there were teasing glimpses into upper-class roots and perhaps the name Maggie. Since the mid-2000s Maw has published a successful series of spin-off books of recipes and remedies. One of these revealed that Maw did of course marry well below her – was it ever in any doubt? – and the other that her name is indeed *Maigret*.

LIVE YOUR LIFE BY MAW

Maw Broon's might be an extreme example, but do you know that in co-habiting heterosexual relationships, studies show that women do around 40 per cent more housework than men and women are almost always the 'default carers' of children? In same-sex partnerships, too, studies suggest that there is not always balance.

Good relationships are based on teamwork. Make sure you take turns at the washing and the washing up. Get a shared calendar and take joint responsibility for taxing the car, arranging dentists' appointments for little people or paying the cleaner. When a kid gets sick at school, take turns in being the one who stays off work.

Make sure you share the good times, too. Find time to sit down together to eat, head out on a date or snuggle up together and watch something you both fancy.

JANET 'JENNIE' LEE

POLITICIAN

I n 2005 the students of the new Adam Smith College in Kirkcaldy refused to name their association after the famous Fife economist, saying that his work is now synonymous with 'exploitation and greed'. Instead, they named themselves after Jennie Lee, a miner's daughter from Lochgelly, for 'the courage and conviction she showed in achieving the aims she believed passionately in'.

Jennie Lee was most definitely her father's daughter. James Lee was fire and safety officer for the pit where he worked in Lochgelly, and an ardent socialist. Jennie inherited his passion for improving the lives of working people in communities like her own, and joined first the Scottish Independent Labour Party and later the Labour Party.

At the University of Edinburgh, Jennie joined the Women's Union and the board of the student newspaper and campaigned to have Bertrand Russell elected as Rector of the University. She trained as a teacher and, after university, taught in Cowdenbeath. In 1929 she won the constituency of North Lanarkshire in a by-election, making her the youngest MP in the Commons. At the time she could not actually vote. The vote had not yet been extended to women under the age of thirty, and Jennie was just twenty-five.

Jennie was indomitable; in her first speech in the Commons she accused Winston Churchill of 'corruption and incompetence'. Churchill was evidently impressed, offering her his congratulations on the speech.

In 1934 Jennie married Aneurin Bevan, the Welsh MP who spearheaded

"Nothing but the best is good enough."

JENNIE LEE
LAYS THE FOUNDATION STONE FOR
THE OPEN UNIVERSITY'S LIBRARY
1973

the establishment of the National Health Service. For a time Jennie's political career was put on hold, but she remained active in many ways, attempting to secure support for the fight against Franco in Spain and supporting the Independent Labour Party when it split from the Labour Party.

Jennie rejoined the Labour Party to stand in Cannock in Staffordshire in 1945 and was elected again to the Commons. She occasionally found herself in opposition to her husband's political beliefs, for example arguing against a UK nuclear deterrent, which Bevan supported.

In 1964 Jennie became the first Minister for the Arts and was key to the establishment of the South Bank Centre in London and the Open University. She delivered a White Paper outlining plans for a 'University of the Air' offering tuition via broadcast and mail, with a place available for anyone who wished to register. She encountered widespread opposition to the plan but she was not a woman to give up and in 1970 the Open University opened. When she died in 1988, she left her papers to the Open University and the collection is held there to this day.

LIVE YOUR LIFE BY JENNIE

Jennie knew all about tenacity. She served in the Commons from 1929 to 1931 and then was not re-elected until 1945, although she stood multiple times. Did she let it get her down? No, she did not. And when it came to the founding of the Open University, she held on through thick and thin, defending her great idea against all comers.

At work, in fitness, in education or in a thousand other areas of life, Jennie's philosophy of hanging on in there is a good one. Dry January and you've fallen off the wagon? Christmas and the gym seems like a distant memory? Exam coming up and you haven't left yourself enough time to revise? Make a plan for what you're going to do to get there and stick to it. That way you can boss anything, just like Jennie.

"'Now,' he says, 'there was a hell of a lot o tinks there, and,' he says, 'they were a gey rauch lot, oh,' he says, 'they were a wild crowd,' he says, 'and my father took me along to see them.' And he looked at me and he said, 'I hope to God you're not one of thae tinks!'"

BELLE STEWART
RECALLS AN EXPERIENCE WITH AN AUDIENCE MEMBER
1977

BELLE STEWART

TRADITION~BEARER

sabella MacGregor was born in a bow tent by the River Tay in 1906, the youngest of three children to survive from a family of nine. Her parents were Highland Scottish Travellers – her father Dan a tinsmith, pearl-fisher and fine ballad singer, and her mother Martha a descendant of a family famed for piping and storytelling. At the time of Belle's birth the family still travelled, but Dan died when she was just months old, and Martha settled in Blairgowrie in the hope of keeping the family together. Belle's years at school were characterised by prejudice towards Travellers, and she spent much of her time picking berries, lifting tatties, making besoms and more. She also accompanied Martha around the farms and villages of Perthshire, hawking small items to make ends meet. She recalled her mother calling them 'pilgrims of the mist' as they set out, hungry, on their travels.

Belle learned family songs and stories from a young age, mastering her first ballad, *The Twa Brithers*, by the age of six. In her late teens she travelled to Ireland to join her mother's relatives pearl-fishing there. Among them was a second cousin, Alec Stewart. Romance blossomed and Belle and Alec married in Ballymoney in 1925, despite family concerns that the closeness of their blood relationship might endanger the health of any children. Happily, their three children were healthy, and they adopted another daughter. For many years they travelled between Ireland and Scotland and many Irish songs made their way into Belle's extensive repertoire.

Belle and Alec lived out their lives together, eventually settling in Blairgowrie and renting a berry field where annual gatherings of Travellers at harvest-time became famous. Belle composed one of her best-loved songs, 'The Berry Fields o Blair', about this key time and place in the lives of many Travellers.

The folklorist Hamish Henderson 'discovered' Belle in the 1950s, realising that her repertoire was unusually extensive and that her voice and style had an intensity of melody Belle called 'the coniach'. Alec, Belle and their daughters Sheila and Cathie would become one of the foremost families in traditional music, beloved of audiences across Scotland and the wider world as the folk revival took flight. Ewan MacColl and Peggy Seeger featured them in a Radio Ballad and wrote a book about them called *'Til Doomsday in the Afternoon.* Another book by daughter Sheila was titled for one of Belle's most famous songs, the 'Queen Amang the Heather'. The song was in many ways synonymous with Belle, and perhaps some feathers were ruffled when fellow Scottish Traveller singer Jeannie Robertson released an album under the name in 1975. In an appropriately queenly manner, Belle simply released her own with the same name in '76. Canadian folklorist Frank Vallee called her 'the most majestic person I have ever seen', and it's not hard to see what he meant.

Belle was a proud and fluent speaker of cant – letters between herself and Alec during the War apparently upset the censors as they could not be checked – and one of a relatively small group of people to perform *canntaireachd*, or bagpipe tunes in syllables performed by a singer. She received a British Empire Medal for services to traditional music and when she died at age ninety-one, she left behind a rich legacy of songs, many of which have found their way into the DNA of Scotland's music.

LIVE YOUR LIFE BY BELLE

Belle's friend Sheila Douglas wrote in an obituary for her, 'Whenever anyone miscalls the travelling people, I think on this wonderful, perceptive, eloquent and gifted lady it has been my privilege to call friend for so many years. No one who knew her could ever look on another traveller through the eyes of prejudice and this is perhaps what we owe to her most of all.'

Belle experienced prejudice all of her life for no reason other than that she belonged to a particular group. She is a powerful reminder that racism, xenophobia and intolerance are problems in all societies across the world.

Instead, you can stand up against prejudice and intolerance and be a human rights champion. There are many places to start: for example, the UK's #fightracism and #Standup4humanrights campaigns.

WITCHES

WITCHES

In the 19th century, American activist and writer Matilda Joslyn Gage came forward with a new theory. The persecution of witches throughout history, she wrote, had nothing to do with fear of the devil or suppression of supernatural evil. Instead it was nothing more than misogyny. Witches were not casters of spells or cavorters with demons. Instead, they were women with specialised knowledge – of the safe delivery of children, perhaps of the *prevention* of children, of herb lore and healing. These women threatened the social order, and so they were to be shut down.

It is true that 'witch' is one of those terms – like 'whore' or 'hag' – that is used *of* a person but rarely *by* that person. And for most of us, the word 'witch' does indeed conjure up the image of a woman. From Macbeth's supernatural advisors to the victims of historic witch panics, and the denizens of Oz to green-faced guisers at Halloween, witches are wifies. From there it's a small step to conclude that wifies, therefore, must be witches. This was Matilda Joslyn Gage's position. As a thought experiment, she suggested that when we see the word 'witches' we should substitute it for 'woman'. Viewed in this way, the history of witches is women's history.

Scotland does have form for charging men with witchcraft – two famous examples were Dr John Fian in 1591 and Major Weir in 1670 – but by far the greatest majority of those prosecuted for witchcraft by the state were women. Unprotected women were especially vulnerable – those without husbands, sons or brothers – together with their sisters on the margins, poor, often elderly and suffering from mental illness or dementia. Maidservants often appear in the records testifying against their friends and acquaintances, reminding us of the hold your boss has over you if you have to live in his house because your job is to wait on his family hand and foot for a pittance that wouldn't support you to live anywhere else. Wise-women, midwives and healers also appear, as do those with juicy property and holdings, often accused by their own nearest and 'dearest' for reasons that are depressingly transparent – at least to the modern eye.

These 'witches' were literally policed by society – arrested, tortured, tried, killed, buried under stones or slabs, occasionally acquitted. The term has also been used to police women in a less literal sense, to undermine them when they exercise power, to challenge them when they step out of line, or to shame them into silence and compliance with socially accepted norms of behaviour. This is true even today and no woman is immune. Mary Queen of Scots was called a 'poisoning witch' in the 1500s; almost four hundred years later Hillary Clinton stood in the 2016 US presidential election and was regularly caricatured online and elsewhere with a pointy hat and green skin.

The green-complexioned, warty, big-nosed model of the evil, aged witch has a long history – witchy hags and crones appear as far back as Ovid, using voodoo dolls and children's organs to cast their spells. In Scotland, the word 'hag' – in Gaelic it's 'cailleach' – has an older resonance. The cailleach was a female creator deity, a weather goddess, an ancestor of all the world. In Scotland we have the Cailleach Bheur, also known as the Queen of Winter. She rules the winter months between Samhainn (Halloween) and Beltane (May Day) and personifies the destructive elements of nature, its storms and its snows. She is credited with shaping Scotland's landscape itself, mountain and loch, and in some stories she renews herself every hundred years with a dip in the icy waters of Loch Bà on Rannoch Moor. She can turn into a bird at will. In one story she tells a shepherd; *Nuair a bha an fhairge ghlas na coill', bha mise nam mhaighdinn òig* – When the ocean was a forest, I was a young girl.

Today there are women all across the world who wish to reclaim the traditions of the goddesses of old and who choose to adopt the term 'witch' for Earth-based belief practices and self-realisation.

In these pages you will find a selection of 'witches' – those actually accused of witchcraft, those more slyly monstered by the term and those who owned their use of female power. You will find openly powerful women and 'bewitchers' who used their power in subtle ways, sharp-tongued critics and wits and quiet thinkers and subverters of convention. Through their stories, let's celebrate female strength; despite the worst efforts to keep us down, our strength will not be diminished and we're certainly not going away.

"Machbet filius Finlach contulit pro suffragiis orationum, et Gruoch filia Bodha, Rex et Regina Scotorum, Kyrkenes, Deo Omnipotenti et Keledeis prefate insule Lochleuine, cum suis finibus et terminis."

"MacBethad son of Findláech and Gruoch daughter of Boite, King and Queen of Scots, granted by the suffrage of prayers Kyrkenes to God the Omnipotent and the Culdees of the Isle of Lochleven, within their bounds and borders."

GRANT OF THE LAND OF KYRKENES
TO THE MONKS OF ST SERFS
12TH-CENTURY LATIN TRANSLATION OF
11TH-CENTURY GAELIC ORIGINAL

GRUOCH OF SCOTLAND

RULER

Gruoch ingean Boite achieves the unusual feat of being a real-life queen almost no one has ever heard of, and simultaneously one of the most famous women in literature.

Gruoch was born into a royal family in a very different Scotland to the one we know today. Her family had ruled the territory called Alba since the time of her great-great-great-grandfather Kenneth MacAlpin, who would pass into legend as having united the Picts and the Scots. She married Gille Coemgáin – try saying that one after a few tequilas – who ruled Moray, the territory to the north of Alba. Gruoch bore a son, Lulach, but Gille Coemgáin was killed in 1032 when the boy was still a child. Gruoch then made a new marriage alliance with her husband's successor – Macbeth. You've probably heard of him.

However, Shakespeare's Lady Macbeth bears little resemblance to the real-life Gruoch. In the play she is a scheming woman who nags and cajoles her weak, ambitious husband to take the throne of Scotland through a series of dark deeds beginning with the murder of Duncan I, King of Scotland, in the dead of night. The reality was less like a plot from *Luther* and more in line with the politics of the Middle Ages. Duncan attacked Macbeth's lands, Macbeth met him in battle and Duncan died in the fight.

Macbeth and Gruoch both had a strong claim to the crown of Scotland, and so they became king and queen together. In an era when the typical reign ended in bloodshed after no more than around five years, they ruled for seventeen. It is an indication of the peace and security of their reign that they were able to make the long journey to Rome on pilgrimage. Gruoch's son Lulach eventually succeeded them.

So why are the events of the play so far from the truth? Gruoch and Macbeth's line died out when Lulach was killed by Malcolm III, and chroniclers scrambled to celebrate Malcolm III's line and demonise Macbeth's. (Think of chroniclers as something akin to Nicholas Witchell in full-on royal correspondent sycophant mode.) Gradually Gruoch was forgotten, along with her claim to the throne of Scotland. Ironically one of the worst demonisers, Andrew de Wyntoun, was a monk on the self-same island to which she and Macbeth had made the grant of Kyrkenes, as quoted above.

Shakespeare read many of these accounts when he wrote *Macbeth* between 1603 and 1607 – over five hundred years after Macbeth and Gruoch ruled Scotland. He was keen to please James VI of Scotland, newly become James I of England. James was ultimately descended from Malcolm, and he had a fervent belief in witches (see page 105), and so Shakespeare wove these elements into his story.

LIVE YOUR LIFE BY GRUOCH

In the world of Facebook and Twitter and all the other myriad social media channels that spring up from nowhere to be ubiquitous in minutes, it can be too easy to dispense with actual human contact. Instead we occupy a world of *he-said-she-said*, badly phrased, wine-fuelled late-night comments and occasional stonking rudeness when it appears that someone we thought we knew has actually lost control of their senses. Next thing we know, we've fallen out with someone based on a conversation we weren't part of when it started and involving at least fifteen people we don't know. Even an email can come across all wrong; who hasn't spent a few minutes of their working day trying to figure out if a colleague or contact is pissed off or not and *why-the-hell-didn't-they-just-put-in-a-crying-with-laughter-emoji-so-you'd-know?!?*

The gap between Gruoch's own life-story and that of her more famous literary incarnation is a salutary lesson in letting people speak for themselves. Step away from the internet feuds and try not to make up your mind about people based on something someone else has said, or from something stupid they've typed in a context that is none of your business anyway. Nine times out of ten it's all a storm in a teacup, whipped up by a social media world designed to encourage you to spend more and more time caught up in its vortex, providing all that rich personal data for sale on to third parties to bankroll the founders' next billion. If an email leaves you stumped, confused or second-guessing its meaning, then why not pick up the phone or walk over to your colleague's desk; some old-fashioned human interaction dispenses with the stress and if it turns out there IS an issue, then hey. You're half way to solving it already.

Shakespeare's Lady Macbeth says, 'What's done, is done.' That's no reason not to try and do better the next time.

"Tha tuille 's
a paidir aig
Gormshuil."

"Gormal
knows more
than her
Paternoster."

MARY MACKELLAR, POET
TELLS TRADITIONS OF GORMAL
1889

GORMSHUIL MHÒR NA MAIGHE
GORMAL OF LOCHABER
WITCH AND ADVISOR

ormal of Lochaber was renowned as the most powerful of a cabal of witches active in the West Highlands and Argyll in the late 1400s and early 1500s. Her fellow witches included the Witch of Jura (special power: turning into a midge) and the Witch of Islay, who had her own Batmobile-esque transport in the form of . . . erm . . . an eggshell in which she could cross the sea. They're like a 1980s children's animation waiting to happen.

Gormal's moniker means 'blue-eyes', but given her witchy credentials we probably shouldn't think 'Sinatra' but rather *one* blue eye and one of another colour. Heterochromia iridium is a good look for anyone; the Gaelic singer Maeve MacKinnon rocks it today and David Bowie totally worked non-matching eyes. Gormal was a cat lady – at a time when felines in the Highlands had a good chance of ending up on a spit, she hung with a pack of them, sought out their wisdom and instructed them to do her will. Anyone who has ever tried to put a cat in a cat basket will appreciate that this is power indeed.

From the above information you *may* have divined that Gormal is remembered in legend as opposed to verifiable historical record – although, in fairness, much historical record relating to witches is even less plausible. She is said to have been a relative of Cameron of Locheil and to have served as an advisor to her chief. If this is true, it was a close relationship – in one story Gormal enlists her cats to help Locheil establish how to do penance for past misdeeds. Her control over cats may relate to the association of cats with the Clan Macintosh, the deadly enemies of the Camerons.

Gormal's story is a tantalising one because it seems to indicate that witches in the Highlands in the Early Modern period could use their supposed powers to their economic and social advantage. Gaelic society certainly believed in seers and in second sight, and Gormal is said to have saved her chief on more than one occasion by warning him of specific dangers such as ambush by rival clans. She is associated with the farm at Moy, near Achnacarry, and may have held this land in payment for services rendered to her chief.

Gormal also pops up in another story with a girl-power element to it. When the Spanish ship *Florencia* moored in the bay in Tobermory, MacLean of Duart is said to have fallen in love with a woman on board. His wife sent for Gormal to neutralise the threat. Gormal turned up with hundreds of cats and instructed them to attack the ship. The cats scrambled aboard, ate the crew and ignited the ship's cargo of gunpowder with sparks from their claws. BOOM!

LIVE YOUR LIFE BY GORMAL

Pets rock. They can lower your blood pressure, combat loneliness, and studies even say that sharing your home with a small furry creature may extend your life. Naturally, it's fine if they're not your bag, but maybe you could make a small donation in cat lady Gormal's memory to a local shelter, the PDSA or similar charity to help an older person or someone on low income experience the very real, life-enhancing pleasure a pet can bring without having to worry about vet bills and other expenses.

MÒR CHAIMBEUL
MARION CAMPBELL
POET AND NOBLEWOMAN

f blood-drinking happens to be your thing, you could do worse than to have been around in the 1500s, an uneasy time in Gaelic Scotland known as *Linn nan Creach* or the Age of Raids. The red stuff spilled all over the place as the clans pursued furious campaigns of looting and pillaging, raiding and murder to supplement their legal – if not particularly humane – actions designed to further their own interests over those of their neighbours. Gradually clan Campbell emerged as the dominant overlords in much of the central and southern Highlands. Marion was born into the branch of the family resident in Glenlyon, the daughter of Donnchadh Ruadh na Fèile, the rather pleasingly named 'Red Duncan the Generous'.

Campbell expansion in the areas around Highland Perthshire had particularly affected the MacGregors, much of whose lands bordered the Campbell territories. For a time the two clans rubbed along together, with the Campbells as overlords and the MacGregors serving them more or less to the benefit of both. Inter-Campbell rivalries and various other factors saw this relationship undermined around 1560. The Campbells of Glenorchy regained control of the ancestral lands of the MacGregors of Glenstrae and imposed hugely toughened conditions on the new young chief, 'Red' Gregor MacGregor. Gregor responded with a series of attacks on the Campbells and a period of conflict ensued.

Evidently there was a brief secession of hostilities around 1565 because Gregor MacGregor of Glenstrae married Marion around this time. What lay behind

"Chuir iad a cheann air ploc daraich
's dhòirt iad fhuil mun làr
Nam biodh agamsa sin copan
dh'òlainn dith mo shàth."

"They put his head on an oak-tree stump
and spilled his blood to the ground
had I had a cup there
I'd have drunk my fill."

MARION CAMPBELL
ON HER HUSBAND'S MURDER
1570

this alliance is not entirely clear, beyond the accepted wisdom that women look for men who remind them of their fathers, as both Duncan and Gregor were redheads. It does appear to have been a love match, and Marion wouldn't be the first young person to enjoy rebelling against their family's wishes where relationships are concerned.

Marion and Gregor wasted no time in starting a family but in 1569, when their first son Alasdair was a baby and Marion was pregnant with their younger son Iain, the Campbells of Glenorchy captured Gregor and imprisoned him at Taymouth. 'Grey' Colin Campbell of Glenorchy and his son Black Duncan of the Skullcap – a charmer who appears in one traditional story murdering a cobbler in revenge for a pair of shoes that blistered his feet – petitioned the crown for permission to put Gregor to death. Eventually they got it. On 7 April 1570, Gregor got the chop; Grey Colin reputedly held the sword. Marion was now a widow with a toddler and a baby son. One can only imagine family gatherings were awkward occasions from thereon in.

In Gaelic society, learned, aristocratic verse was not an equal opps profession (see page 173), but Marion was a noblewoman and would have been well acquainted with poetry as a listener. She used this knowledge to make a wild lament for her husband, framed as a lullaby to her infant son. It is still sung today, having survived in oral tradition for a remarkable three hundred years until it was first written down around 1890. This survival is testament to Marion's skill as a poet, and to the power of her emotions. It is a song of love and hate, brimming with praise for Gregor and spitting curses at Marion's own Campbell kin. Grief and anger scream in every line as she relates how she has torn her own hair and skin and wishes she had been present at the execution to taste some of that sweet MacGregor blood. Bleurgh.

LIVE YOUR LIFE BY MARION

Whatever else she might have been, Marion was determined. She had really, really set her heart on something, and she pushed back against it all to have it – family, clan and accepted gender hierarchies. Thanks to the time at which she lived, she paid a miserable price. But her words are still with us, a testament to a voice that would not be silenced.

Many of the singers who passed Marion's song down through the generations were other women, helping to preserve the words of a sister whose spirit, feistiness and refusal to yield struck a spark in them too. You can find strength in other women's words and stories – not just those in this book, but in biography and fiction and art and film. Seek out books and films of women's stories, and gift them to your daughters and your sisters and, even more importantly, to your sons and brothers, male partners and male friends. For far too long the books, films and plays of the West have prioritised men's voices over women's and we've become so used to it that we don't think to challenge it. Even today a terrifying proportion of Hollywood films fail the 'Bechdel test', a simple exercise of three questions: *Is there more than one woman in this? Do they have names? Do they talk to each other about something other than a man?* If the answer is 'no', we don't have to provide an audience.

Don't be afraid either to add your own voice to the throng. Find a writing group, keep a journal, whatever you fancy. It can help empty your mind at the end of the day, work through anything that's bothering you or stretch your creative talents as you imagine new worlds or how it might feel to walk a mile in someone else's shoes.

MARY STUART
QUEEN OF SCOTS
RULER

Mary Stuart is often dismissed as politically naïve and ruled by passions. From a modern perspective, she actually looks suspiciously like that mate of yours who is a perfectly good and competent person, even brilliant on occasion, but for some reason goes out with a succession of complete and utter dickheads. In your mate's case it can be almost impossible to understand. Is it low self-esteem? Does her dad treat her mum like that? Has she just been worn down by dickheads 1, 2 and 3? *Are there even any decent men in the world?!?!*

From a distance of over four hundred years, we have even less chance of understanding Mary's motivations – not that many biographers haven't tried – but one thing is certain. She was operating under the added pressure that she needed a man to ensure a succession of the royal kind.*

Mary had a distinctly cheerless start in life, born as her father James V lay on his deathbed. She was his only child born in wedlock, and succeeded to the crown of Scotland at just six days old. Her French mother was keen to seal the alliance between France and Scotland and Mary was promptly packed off to be raised at the French court. Her education there gave her a mastery of French, Italian, Latin, Spanish, Greek and Scots, the ability to play the lute and the virginals, a particular talent for needlework and a love of horse riding and falconry. She grew into a tall young woman, and one considered especially attractive by

* *Royal successions and successions of dickheads are not mutually exclusive.*

"I forgive you
with all my heart,
for now, I hope,
you shall make
an end
of all my
troubles."

TRADITIONAL WORDS OF MARY QUEEN OF SCOTS
PARDONING HER EXECUTIONER
1587

the ideas of the time. Naturally this meant she was married at sixteen to the short, stuttering Francis, Dauphin of France. In 1559 the couple ascended to the French throne. Francis didn't live long enough to say whether he'd have turned out to be a dickhead; in 1560 the poor lad died of an ear infection that resulted in an abscess in his brain.

There was little time to grieve for Francis – Mary was soon off home to Scotland, a place she had not seen since she was five years old. It was time to take up her throne as a devout Catholic in a country in the grip of the Protestant Reformation. Initially she navigated the dangerous and complex political situation relatively well, permitting religious freedom and appointing Protestant Lords as close advisors. She survived a lot of thundering verbal attacks from the pulpit, two bedroom invasions and one uprising, but did not succeed in finding a husband from the limited gene pool of European royalty. Instead she settled on her own cousin Henry, Lord Darnley, who was in possession – as was Mary – of a claim to the English throne. The cousins had originally met when Henry's parents had sent him to France to try his chances with Mary after Francis's death. Classy move, huh?

The Darnley marriage produced a male heir, James, but otherwise was a disaster. It seems that Darnley couldn't cope with the power balance in the marriage (surprise!) or with Mary's friendship with her private secretary, Rizzio. He could do nothing about the former – Mary refused to name him her co-ruler and her automatic successor – and so he fixed on the latter, killing Rizzio in front of a pregnant Mary. What a guy.

The following year Darnley was assassinated and Mary's troubles began in earnest. She was suspected of ordering the murder, and was soon after abducted by the most likely suspect in the case, the Earl of Bothwell. Accounts vary as to whether Mary had agreed to the abduction as a ruse, or whether Bothwell simply wished to force himself on the Queen. Bothwell obtained a quickie divorce from his wife – one of the perks of Protestantism – and married Mary, who may have been pregnant, as sources say she later miscarried twins.

The Bothwell marriage was deeply unpopular but sadly not in a *what-you-doin'-sister?* kind of a way. An alliance of Scottish lords rode out against the couple, meeting Mary, Bothwell and her army at Carberry Hill in East Lothian. Bothwell was escorted from the field and sent into exile and Mary was imprisoned and forced to abdicate. Ever a trier, she escaped from her prison and raised an army but was defeated and fled to England where she threw herself on the tender mercies of her cousin Elizabeth I. And by tender mercies, I mean eighteen years in captivity, followed by a date with an axeman who missed on the first attempt and finished the job by sawing at the sinews of her neck until her head finally came off. She was forty-four years old.

Mary was divisive in her lifetime, and in the centuries since her death she has been painted variously as a silly schemer, a tragic heroine, a Catholic martyr, a beautiful bewitcher of men, a victim of her time and gender, a tolerant young ruler doing her best in the face of impossible odds, and a queen who had, in a sense, the last laugh when her son succeeded to the throne of England. It's often forgotten that she was one of the best-known women writers of her era – so much so that her enemies attempted to discredit her by circulating scandalous work under her name. Her poems and letters reveal skill, elegance and dignity.

On the eve of her execution, Mary wrote:

> Oh my enemies, set your envy all aside;
> I've no more eagerness for high domain;
> I've borne too long the burden of my pain
> To see your anger swiftly satisfied.
> And you, my friends who have loved me so true,
> Remember, lacking health and heart and peace,
> there is nothing worthwhile I can do;
> ask only that my misery should cease
> And that, being punished in a world like this,
> I have my portion of eternal bliss.

LIVE YOUR LIFE BY MARY

Be inspired by Mary's *bad* example by not marrying, moving in with or otherwise giving over any portion of your precious independence to a dickhead. That should go without saying but now, as then, it happens.

So how do you recognise one? Here are some suggestions and potential actions to neutralise any situations you have wandered into while blinded by lust/a nice Match profile pic/tequila.

- Your friends aren't saying anything but it's kinda clear they think your new partner's an arse. What do they know anyway? Erm . . . you. They have no motivation except caring for you. Hint: listen to your crew, have a think about the behaviours they are seeing and why your friends might be responding in the way that they are. You might thank them in the long run.
- He lets his disappointment be known if you choose not to sleep with him on a first date. Hint: don't go on a second one.
- If he pays, he expects something else in return. Sex should never be a transaction, or something you 'owe'.
- He makes you feel that you need to change something. You do. Him.

('he' is not used here to imply issues of control don't apply in same-sex relationships too, but societal conditioning of males is such that many of these problems are massively men-on-women ones.)

"Euphame MacCalzean, as culpable and guilty thereof, to be taken to the castle hill of Edinburgh and there bound to the stake and burned in ashes, quick to the death and all and sundry her lands, heritages, tacks, steadings, rooms, possessions, corns, cattle, goods and gear to be forfeited and escheat to our sovereign lord's use. "

SENTENCE IS PASSED ON
EUPHAME MACCALZEAN
1591

EUPHAME MACCALZEAN
(PRONOUNCED 'MACLEAN')
'WITCH'

Euphame MacCalzean had the great misfortune of being around during a period when the latest big craze wasn't adult colouring books or contouring. Instead it was torturing and killing people in all manner of evil ways in the name of safeguarding society from . . . evil. The bad kind of evil, aka witchcraft.

As with all good crazes, Scotland's first witch persecution began with the celebrities of the day. King James VI had recently travelled to Copenhagen to marry Princess Anne of Denmark. On the way home, the royal couple were beset by terrible storms and forced to take shelter in Norway for several weeks. Transport delays resulted in outcry then as now, and the admiral of the Danish fleet was keen to find someone to blame. He quickly pointed the finger at the wife of a high official in Copenhagen, on the basis that he had recently insulted her. Talk about transference.

This grave accusation resulted in a witch panic in Denmark and a number of women confessed to having used sorcery to raise the storms that beset Queen Anne's ship. Two were ultimately burned as witches. When King James heard of this, he determined to set up his own tribunal and settled on the Scottish seaside town of North Berwick, where a maid called Geillis Duncan conveniently – for James, not for Geillis or any of her associates – confessed to her master David Seton that she had been up to various storm-raising activities and other malevolence.

Over a hundred suspected witches were arrested in North Berwick and liberal application of torture saw many of them confess. James was a hands-on sort of chap and he personally interrogated one of the women – Agnes Sampson – who broke after severe physical torture. A pamphlet called *Newes from Scotland* kept the public up-to-speed with the latest burnings. Think the *Daily Mail* Sidebar of Shame with added religious paranoia.

Euphame MacCalzean was one of the women accused by Geillis Duncan, and her case is an interesting one from a modern perspective. Euphame was the daughter of Thomas MacCalzean, Lord Cliftonhall, an eminent Edinburgh lawyer. Euphame was Cliftonhall's only child, and he recognised her as his legal heir in 1558. Euphame married another lawman, Patrick Moscrop, but retained her own name, perhaps as an indication of her elevated status relative to her husband. They had at least five children and Patrick took Euphame's surname. This distinctly modern-sounding move was not an indicator of a happy marriage – Patrick had left Euphame and gone to France before she was accused.

When Geillis Duncan named Euphame as an accomplice in devil-worship, prosecutors jumped on the MacCalzean/Moscrop marriage to paint Euphame as a controlling woman using magic to bend her husband to her will. She was accused of trying to bring about the deaths of her husband, his father and the extended Moscrop family, and *actually* bringing about the deaths of her cousin and her nephew. She was also accused of the diabolical action of relieving the pain of women in childbirth, which sounds pretty good to the modern ear but to the misogynists of the Early Modern period represented an attempt to interfere with God's plan to cause women as much misery as possible.

Newes from Scotland is depressingly silent on some pertinent facts relating to Euphame. Geillis Duncan's master David Seton – he who reported the original accusations – was married to Euphame's sister-in-law Katherine Moscrop. The two families had quarrelled over the portions of Katherine and Patrick Moscrop's father's estate which each had received on his death. Other members of the extended family who jumped in with their own accusations may have hoped to gain from Euphame's death – in fact, one accuser had previously tried to sue on the basis that he should have inherited her father's property instead of her.

Modern research suggests that women without husbands, sons or brothers were most likely to be accused of witchcraft, and thereafter more likely to be tried and executed. Euphame had none of these at the time of her arrest – she was her father's only heir and her surviving children were three daughters named as her own successors. Her husband was in France, supposedly having fled in fear of his wife. Euphame was in charge of her own fortune and looking like a serious threat to the social order of the day.

Today Edinburgh's Castle Hill is packed with tourists admiring the views across the city from the Esplanade, heading up to the Castle or down to the Camera Obscura, or browsing seemingly endless displays of tacky tartan souvenirs. Back in Euphame MacCalzean's day it had a more sinister resonance as the place where witches were put to death. Euphame was taken there in 1591. In her death sentence, replicated at the beginning of this story, the word 'quick' doesn't mean 'speedy'. It means 'alive'. Euphame was burned without even the small mercy of being strangled first.

Euphame was not without friends; after her death several continued to seek to clear her name. David Ogilvy, who spoke for Euphame at her trial, obtained permission to speak with Geillis Duncan before her own execution. Geillis told Ogilvy she had never even met Euphame. A year after her death, James VI (now also James I) expunged Euphame's record and returned her property to her family. In doing so, he imposed the status quo in terms of gender roles – Euphame's husband was named administrator for his daughters, with any husbands they married taking on the same role. Her daughter Martha was by this time married to the very same David Ogilvy who had advocated for Euphame. He and the Moscrops now controlled her substantial property. The gender hierarchy was firmly back in place.

LIVE YOUR LIFE BY EUPHAME

Many Scottish witches suffered because they were women. Euphame suffered because she had stuff other people wanted. She was wealthy in a way that was a threat to the social order, because/and she was a woman. Bye, bye, Euphame.

This maps across in some ways to the modern concept of intersectionality – the fact that people can suffer discrimination not because of one factor or another, but because of the interaction of two or more. So a black woman may struggle to find a job with an employer who employs both black people and women, because the black employees are all men working on the shop floor, and the woman employees are all white, working in the office. There is no place for the black woman because of her combination of blackness and femaleness.

Be alert to intersectionality, and as part of that awareness, remember that people have specific circumstances and experiences and try to refrain from the sort of thinking that says, 'I come from X background, and I've made good, so why should I have any time for a person who comes from a similar one but is having a rough time?' Try instead to count your own blessings and aim to help others if you can, as opposed to censuring. If you can't do anything or don't want to, zip your lip and walk on by without judgement. As they used to say, if you can't say anything nice, don't say anything at all.

JANET WISHART

'WITCH'

I t was the late 1500s, video content hadn't been invented yet, and people had to make their own entertainment. Janet Wishart was presumably doing just this in 1572 when she was spotted leaving the yard of her neighbour Adam Mair in Aberdeen one night around 2 a.m. So far, so *Hollyoaks*. But by 1597 the Second Scottish Witch Hunt was in full swing, and Adam Mair's wife saw her chance for revenge. Upon being discovered in the Mairs' yard by a group of students, she claimed, Janet Wishart cursed the lads in fury. By the next afternoon two of the students were dead, drowned in the Auld Wattergang on the Links.

Janet was taken up, accused of thirty-one counts of witchcraft in total over a span of twenty-four years. These ranged from raising storms by means of throwing out live coals from her fire, to inducing alternating shivering fits and fevers in her victims (aka 'the flu'). She was also accused of using her 'nightmare cats' to terrify neighbours into having bad dreams – a claim any cat owner will immediately recognise as the unenlightened prejudice of the cat-hater. One peculiarly satisfying charge was that she stopped her daughter's husband from hitting her, whereupon the poor son-in-law was attacked by a dog. Most damningly of all – brace yourself – Janet was accused of dancing and playing music at the Fish Cross in Aberdeen. Imagine!

To the modern eye these charges appear ridiculous but Janet was tried in great earnest by the local court, with the blessing of a royal commission. Joining her in court were her husband John Leys, their son, their daughters and a woman

"Weill haif ye schemit me. I sail gar the best of yow repent."

JANET WISHART'S
THREAT TO STUDENTS IN ADAM MAIR'S YARD
IN 1572, AS LATER REPORTED

called Isobel Cockie. Janet's daughter Violet was accused of cutting parts off a hanged corpse.

Janet was found guilty on eighteen counts of witchcraft. She and Isobel Cockie – whose supposed crimes have been lost to history – were burned at the stake, with Janet's death costing Aberdeen eleven pounds and ten shillings for the executioner's fee, peat, tar barrels and coals. Her son suffered the same fate, but her husband and daughters were acquitted. They were banned from Aberdeen due to their association with Janet. Whatever your own take on the Granite City, it's hard to imagine the remaining members of Janet's family had much affection left for it by that point in any case.

LIVE YOUR LIFE BY JANET

The price Janet paid for, essentially, being out at night seems disproportionate in the extreme. That said, those of us who live in cities may on occasion have fantasised about violent reprisals for drunk students fighting on the streets in the wee small hours, neighbours partying till 4 a.m. on a school night or that guy down the road who cuts his hedge with a chainsaw at 7 a.m. on a Sunday morning.

Don't be those people. Some of the people you disturb have buses to drive, train tracks to weld or anaesthetics to administer, and it really is best that they do it on some sleep.

"Bha mi uair nach do shaoil mi
Gus an do chaochail air m' aimsir
Gun tiginn an taobh seo
Dh'amharc Dhiùraidh à Sgarbaidh."

"Once I would never have thought
until circumstances changed so far
that I would come here to Scarba,
to look over to Jura."

MARY MACLEOD ON HER EXILE

MÀIRI NIGHEAN ALASDAIR RUAIDH
MARY MACLEOD
POET AND NURSEMAID

Mary was born in Rodel in Harris around 1600, and spent much of her life in Dunvegan on the Isle of Skye. She lived in the home of the MacLeods of Harris and Dunvegan, where she was nursemaid to generations of chiefs. She was also a brilliant poet.

Poetry plays a hugely important part in Gaelic culture, where it has always been much more than pretty words designed to give pleasure or pause for thought to the listener. In Gaelic society, poetry was power. Poets were advisers to their chiefs, lawmakers and judges, and perhaps in the more distant past magicians or seers too. In the 1100s the poet Muireadhach Ó Dálaigh considered himself so important in the clan ecosystem that he killed a rent-collector when the man insulted him by asking him to pay up. To Muireadhach's mind, he had already paid in full, delivering poetry in support of his chief and clan that functioned a little like modern spin, promoting clan and national interests. He may also have believed that he could continue rent-free for fear of the harm he might do with his words. Six hundred years later another angry poet makes an unpleasant threat that shows just how dangerous a poet's words were believed to be:

> De dh' òirlichean aoiridh bàrdail,
> toiseam o d' bhathais, gu d' shàil thu;
> 'S feannam do leathar a thràill dhiot . . .

With satirical poetic inches,
I will take the measure of you from forehead to feet;
and I will flay your skin from you, wretch . . .

Poets were powerful people indeed and poetry was important work. As such, it was considered the preserve of – you've guessed it – men. Women made songs and ditties – if a task's worth doing in Gaelic Scotland, it deserves a song to go with it – but these were personal songs of love and loss, praise poems to men of the normal kind, not great blasts of the war-trumpet in support of chiefs or kings. Little songs, for private spaces. The big stuff was for public performance, and for men.

Mary broke these rules. She made praise poems to important men, particularly Norman MacLeod of Berneray, a cousin of MacLeod of MacLeod. The story goes that she was told to stop, to make no new poetry inside (i.e. in the women's world) or outside (in the men's). What did Mary do? She stood on the threshold and carried on.

Mary's poetry continued to get her into trouble. She was exiled for a time to the small island of Scarba, across the Corryvreckan whirlpool from the Isle of Jura, where she made the song quoted on page 112. No records survive to explain why she was exiled, but tradition says she was too effusive in her praise for Sir Norman of Berneray and so offended MacLeod of MacLeod. Eventually, she was brought back to Dunvegan and continued to make her poems.

Today Mary is considered in the context of an important group of poets who had begun to compose work in Scottish Gaelic, as opposed to the Classical language of the trained bards – an artificial literary language common to Scotland and Ireland, preserved by bardic schools where poets learned their trade. Few of her works remain but those we have are very fine.

It seems safe to say that Mary was less respected in her own day. Tradition has it that she was put in her grave according to the Norse custom for burying a witch, facedown under a pile of stones. The lengths they'll go to to keep a strong woman down!

LIVE YOUR LIFE BY MARY

Whether or not you subscribe to the specific belief that words can actually take the skin off a person, there's no denying that they have power. Try to be thoughtful in your choice of words, and especially avoid using terms that can hurt. Language can denigrate, bully and perpetuate inequality – think of the way 'girl' is used as in insult when a man or boy is afraid or upset – or it can empower, uplift and inspire. It's up to you how you choose to use it.

This has a specific resonance in the present day, particularly in spaces and places where traditional definitions of gender are interrogated. One result of changing perceptions and understanding is that language around sex and gender has become highly loaded.

In this discussion – and others – we should respect the power of language. Particularly we should respect individuals' preferences when it comes to the words they use to define themselves. These are highly personal, and any individual has the right to ask not to be called a name that they do not believe is theirs.

"Marriage or death.
Remember whose daughter
I am!"

RACHEL CHIESLEY
LADY GRANGE
PRISONER

I f a settled home life is conducive to a happy adulthood, Rachel Chiesley never stood a chance. She was one of ten children born to John Chiesley and his wife Margaret Nicholson in Dalry House on the western side of Edinburgh. In 1688, when Rachel was nine years old, her mother divorced her father and successfully sued him for 'aliment' in the sum of 1,700 merks to support herself and the children. It wasn't a lot of money, but John Chiesley was furious nonetheless. The following Easter, he shot and killed George Lockhart of Carnwath, the judge in the case, in front of a crowd of witnesses. Chiesley was taken up and tried, with added torture permitted by a special dispensation from Parliament to the Edinburgh magistrates. The thinking was that Chiesley might give up the names of some accomplices when the thumbscrews came out. It seems, however, that while Lockhart's death may have been politically expedient to some in Scotland, Chiesley was mainly just one of those shits that don't want to pay maintenance and will go to any lengths to avoid it.

Chiesley was hanged three days after his crime, minus the hand that had held the pistol. It was chopped off while he was still alive and hung around his neck with the offending weapon for the drop. Margaret buried him in an unmarked grave and found herself no longer in need of aliment as she and the children now had it all.

Daughter Rachel grew into something of a beauty with a wild reputation she perhaps cultivated just a *leetle bit*. Tradition has it that her marriage was a shotgun affair – literally, as she is said to have threatened her intended with a pistol – and there were rumours that she continued to sleep with a razorblade under her pillow just to add a little spice to proceedings. Her lucky bridegroom was Lord Grange, the brother of 'Bobbing' John, Earl of Mar. The Earl had bobbed over to the losing side in the 1715 Jacobite Rising and had been stripped of his lands and exiled for his trouble. Lord Grange was also a Jacobite, but he was a secret one – the safest kind to be at the time, as were many of his friends, too. He must have been a pretty good actor – he rose to become Lord Advocate and later a Member of Parliament, like a good Hanoverian with no Jacobite leanings whatsoever.

Violent tendencies and large families perhaps ran in the Chiesley line, as Rachel and her husband had four sons and five daughters. They lived for twenty-five years in 'great peace' as she recalled in a letter, but John was serially unfaithful and Rachel a spendthrift with a fondness for a tipple. The marriage soured and in 1731 or '32 Rachel apparently threatened to expose her husband's more secret political leanings. A gang of men broke into her house, a violent scuffle ensued, and Rachel disappeared. Lord Grange regretfully let it be understood that his wife was dead.

Said wife was, in truth, very alive and literally kicking as she was transported across the country by her husband's network of conspirators. She was held first on Heisker in the Monach Islands off North Uist and then on St Kilda in conditions that seemed miserable in the extreme to a pampered Edinburgh lady without any ability to communicate in Gaelic. We know all this because Rachel managed to smuggle a letter from St Kilda to Edinburgh in 1738 (it took a mere two years to arrive). Scandal ensued and her lawyer, Thomas Hope of Rankeillor, dispatched a force to search for her. Lord Grange still maintained that *she was dead, that was his story and he was sticking to it, and look, it was definitely true and not a lie at all as he had had a funeral for her and everything.* In fairness, the guy had told so many fibs that even he might have forgotten what the truth really was.

Lady Grange was spirited away from St Kilda to mainland Scotland and then to Skye, where she died – still in captivity – in 1745. She was buried at Trumpan with a later show funeral at Duirinish for reasons that are unclear today but have an uncomfortable echo of the various fusses made over the burial of witches. Her husband carried on womanising and paid no great price for either his secret Jacobite leanings or his appalling treatment of his wife. A number of his co-conspirators fared less well – Simon Fraser, Lord Lovat, the likely mastermind of the kidnap plot, lost his head on Tower Hill.

LIVE YOUR LIFE BY RACHEL

The whole miserable story of Rachel's life might have been averted had her father had a grown-up chat with her mother about appropriate levels of maintenance for a woman and ten children after a divorce. Instead he got all het up about his rights, forgetting that responsibilities also dictate how we should live our lives.

If you go through a break-up involving children – and many of us will – think of Rachel and try your damnedest to keep things amicable at best and civil at worst. However hard your ex pushes you – and God knows exes know how – keep the kids clear of it. This may involve biting your tongue when confronted by gems such as 'my daddy's bought me a iPad so when I wake up in the night at his house I can play my videos'.

If your ex really, really won't engage with the kids' needs and agree strategies with you to ensure they are consistently and appropriately parented regardless of location, then the best you can do is ensure your own home is a calm place with firm rules everyone understands.

"I am at this moment ready to hang myself for a young Edinburgh widow, who has wit and beauty more murderously fatal than the assassinating stiletto of the Sicilian Banditti."

ROBERT BURNS WRITES TO
HIS FRIEND RICHARD BROWN OF
AGNES MACLEHOSE
1789

AGNES MACLEHOSE

MUSE

gnes 'Nancy' Craig was born in Glasgow in 1758. The sickly child of a surgeon and a minister's daughter, she grew up with a strong religious belief and a keen interest in books.

By her teens Nancy had recovered and was by all accounts both exceptionally good-looking and a good conversationalist for an era in which few women had the chance to read. She soon caught the eye of a Glasgow lawyer named James Maclehose and although her family disapproved of him, Maclehose was determined. Upon discovering that Nancy was to travel to Edinburgh, he infamously booked all other seats in the coach in order to have the chance of speaking with her alone. Despite her family's objections, she married him in 1776, at the age of eighteen.

Four children followed in four years, but the Maclehose marriage was not a happy one. Before the birth of her fourth child, Nancy left her husband, citing his cruelty and depressive tendencies. Maclehose spent a time in a debtors' prison before sailing for Jamaica in 1782. Before he left he wrote to ask her to accompany him. 'I am willing to forget what is past,' he offered, 'neither do I require an apology from you.' Nancy refused, but the price was high – Maclehose took custody of their sons.

Nancy's father died in 1782, and she took a small flat in Edinburgh where she eked out a living with the help of wealthier relations. In 1787 she attended a tea party with Robert Burns, who was then the toast of the town. Nancy wrote Burns a note inviting him to visit her the following week. Burns had an accident that prevented the visit; the pair instead began a correspondence filled with passion and longing, fantasy and nonsense. Using the name 'Sylvander', Burns professed his love for 'Clarinda'; Nancy wrote back:

> Talk not of Love, it gives me pain,
> For Love has been my foe;
> He bound me with an iron chain.
> And plunged me deep in woe . . .
> Your Friendship much can make me blest,
> O, why that bliss destroy!
> Why urge the odious, one request
> You know I must deny!

Nancy's relationship with Burns was never, it seems, a physical one despite his best efforts. He turned his attentions instead to her servant Jenny Clow, who bore him a son, and to a girl named May Cameron, and eventually he returned to Jean Armour, who was also pregnant by him. He married Jean six weeks after writing to Nancy to assure her that Jean was, compared to her, *a farthing taper beside the cloudless glory of the meridian sun'*.

Nancy's wealthier relations were concerned to protect her reputation; perhaps it was under their advice that she sailed to Jamaica in 1791 to attempt to reconcile with her husband. She remembered her last parting with Burns as a pitiful one, and he commemorated it with *Ae Fond Kiss*, one of his most famous and loveliest songs.

Nancy arrived in Jamaica to find James Maclehose ensconced in a slave plantation with one of his slaves as a mistress. She sailed home to Scotland by return and lived out her life in Edinburgh, eventually regaining custody of her sons. In her old age she enjoyed the fame of her correspondence with Burns, controlling access to their letters with some style. She even had tea with Jean Armour, when they talked at length about their families and their shared affection for the long-dead Burns.

LIVE YOUR LIFE BY AGNES

Within the strict and anti-woman structures of her day, Nancy very much controlled her own story. She enjoyed a long friendship/flirtation with Burns, and it is worth noting that she still adored the man many years after his death. It's questionable whether any of the women who tumbled into bed with him felt so fondly, and isn't that a thought worth pondering?

"Two bright blue eyes that gleamed with a lustre like that of insanity, an utterance of astonishing rapidity, a nose and chin that almost met together, and a ghastly expression of cunning . . ."

WALTER SCOTT DESCRIBES
BESSIE MILLAR
1814

BESSIE MILLAR

ENTREPRENEUR

S ir Walter Scott was a terrible visitor. As well as his comments on Bessie Millar's appearance, he had unkind words for the 'dirty and precipitous lanes' that led up to her home on the brow of Brinkies Brae in Stromness on the mainland of Orkney. Bessie was nearly one hundred years old, she told Scott, and many hundreds of feet had tramped those lanes to her door. What they sought, and Bessie sold, was the favour of the wind.

Orkney is a seafaring place and favourable winds were key to whether a sailor would return home on time, late . . . or not at all. To give themselves the best possible chance of a good voyage, seamen would 'buy the wind' – three knots of thread, rope or fabric they could undo whenever a particular wind was required. The third knot was never to be undone, for it unlocked a hurricane.

Witches had long been said to be able to raise – and calm – storms. Many wise women saw the commercial potential in this belief and began to 'sell the wind' to mariners across Scandinavia and northern parts of Scotland in the 18th century. Meg Watt in Duncansby catered to the sailors of Caithness. In Orkney, men and boys climbed that steep Stromness brae and tramped to the door of Bessie Millar, as did Walter Scott. He was seeking not a safe voyage, but inspiration for his writing among Scotland's traditions, and Bessie would make her own way into his novel *The Pirate* in 1822.

Bessie laid no claim to witchcraft and she did not deal in knots, although her rival Stromness wind-seller, Mammie Scott, did, using red thread for added drama. Instead, Bessie took a fee of sixpence, boiled her kettle and said a prayer, and this blessing protected the sailor for his forthcoming voyage. Why she particularly had the reputation of influencing the wind is lost to us, but evidently Bessie saw no conflict between her professed Christian faith and the small fee she charged for her services.

The tradition of 'buying the wind' travelled across the Atlantic and is recorded in Newfoundland and Labrador as late as the 1970s.

LIVE YOUR LIFE BY BESSIE

Bessie didn't have much, and so she made the most of what she had. She also knew the power of a cup of tea. Many of us today spend a large proportion of our limited readies on take-away coffees and teas, and along the way create a mountain of plastic, paper and wooden stirrers that contribute to the many woes of the planet. Make a resolution to get yourself a keep-cup, a flask, a reusable coffee filter and a box of tea-bags, and set yourself a target to make your refreshing hot beverages at home or in the office instead of popping into your coffee chain of choice. Every time you make yourself a coffee or tea instead of buying one, pop the money you've saved into a jar and when you have a nice little fund, treat yourself to something nice or make a donation to a worthy cause.

JANE WELSH CARLYLE

WRITER

Jane Baillie Welsh was born in Haddington in 1801 and married aspiring writer Thomas Carlyle at the age of twenty-five in 1826. Jane was a doctor's daughter, a much-adored only child and a talented writer in her own right. Her mother was said to have considered her daughter a cut above her suitor, and indeed Thomas was both less privileged and considerably more tortured when it came to producing the works of literary genius to which he aspired. In fairness, six-volume histories can take a while to produce, especially when written longhand.

When the couple moved to London in the hope of advancing Thomas's writing career, Jane proved invaluable as a wise and witty hostess, welcoming many figures of the literary establishment into their home. So highly was she regarded that it was believed for a time that she was the true author of *Jane Eyre*.

Eventually Thomas found the success the Carlyles sought and came to be considered the leading social critic of Victorian England. While Jane's support for his career was unfailing, in many ways the Carlyle marriage was not a success. The novelist Samuel Butler once quipped, 'It was very good of God to let Carlyle and Mrs Carlyle marry one another, and so make only two people miserable and not four.' Thousands of letters between the two reveal their tempestuous relationship. There were no children and a third party in the marriage in the form of society hostess Lady Ashburn, with whom Thomas became obsessed, causing Jane to contemplate suicide. Thomas was also fond of metaphors relating to excrement in his writing and discussions of his bowels in life. Jane wrote in

"Oh Lord! If you but knew what a brimstone of a creature I am behind all this beautiful amiability!"

JANE WELSH CARLYLE
WRITES TO ELIZA STODART
1836

1834, 'I am more and more persuaded that there is no complete misery in the world that does not emanate from the bowels,' putting herself ahead of medical science by generations.

Jane found rather more fulfillment – if not contentment – in her friendship with the writer Geraldine Jewsbery, who wrote to her, 'I feel towards you much more like a lover than a female friend.' Some of her literary ambitions found an outlet in helping shape her friend's work, but this too was a tempestuous relationship with regular fallings-out and jealousies.

When Jane died at just sixty-four, Thomas was deeply distressed and wrote a highly self-critical memoir, *Reminiscences of Jane Welsh Carlyle*. The work was published after Thomas's death and gave rise to widespread speculation that the marriage was never consummated. Virginia Woolf joined in the controversy, suggesting that Jane's relationship with Geraldine Jewsbery was indeed a romantic one.

LIVE YOUR LIFE BY JANE

While Jane's frustrated literary talent has been ascribed to her difficult personal circumstances, others have noted that other female writers of her era overcame significant obstacles, and few of those women enjoyed the literary connections Jane had. She was an incredibly prolific and talented letter-writer; perhaps she did not seek an outlet beyond that.

At Jane's time, marriage could be a barrier to women living their own lives. Take inspiration from Jane and don't let your relationship steal your ambitions. You can, and should, have your own life – one of fulfilment, creativity, joy and self-actualisation – within any proper partnership.

"Margaret has genius, I have only talent."

CHARLES RENNIE MACKINTOSH ON
MARGARET MACDONALD MACKINTOSH

MARGARET MACDONALD MACKINTOSH

ARTIST

Behind every man, they say, is a good woman. Charles Rennie Mackintosh was cleverer than that; he might have used the word 'beside'. He happily acknowledged that half of 'his' work was his wife's. In fact, he once wrote, she could claim three quarters of it.

Margaret Macdonald was born near Wolverhampton in 1864. Her father was originally from Glasgow and the family moved back north, into a grand house on an estate her father managed. Legend had it that the house stood on the site of an ancient stone circle or Celtic site. In 1890 Margaret enrolled at the Glasgow School of Art, as did her sister Frances, to study design. The sisters were especially interested in Celtic images, symbolism and folklore and their approach was fluid and imaginative, organic and stylised. Their work encompassed metalwork, embroidery, textiles and large panels in gesso – a compound based on plaster of Paris which they spread and piped onto panels to create raised and textured designed they painted and set with stones and glass. Surreally, an observer likened their gesso technique to icing a cake.

At the School of Art Frances and Margaret met up-and-coming architect Charles Rennie Mackintosh – they called him 'Toshie' – and Herbert MacNair, who were both enrolled as night students. Soon 'the Four' were exhibiting together. They had a distinct style featuring elongated, spectral forms and many in Glasgow mocked them as 'The Spook School'. But as the Four's work developed, it played a key part in placing Glasgow at the centre of fashion. Soon much of Europe was coveting 'the Glasgow Style'.

In 1900 Margaret and Toshie married and began to collaborate on buildings, some real and some imagined, for exhibitions and competitions. When Toshie received a commission he insisted on complete control of both exterior and interior; Margaret had a significant hand in the intricate interior schemes and contributed many of the artworks displayed within them. The Mackintoshes' exhibition at the Vienna Succession in the year of their marriage was an influence on figures including Gustav Klimt – he of *The Kiss*, replicated on student bedroom walls across the world in the 1990s.

The Mackintoshes' reputation in Vienna far outstripped the commissions they received at home in the UK. The couple made plans to relocate there, but war intervened. Instead they made their way to Suffolk and eventually to France. They returned to London when Toshie became ill – he died of cancer in 1928 and Margaret followed him in 1933.

No work by Margaret survives after 1921. Both of the Mackintoshes enjoyed early success but afterwards were under-appreciated in their lifetimes. Many of their interior schemes were broken up and destroyed or placed into storage and forgotten.

Today Charles Rennie Mackintosh is probably Scotland's most famous architect and one of our most famous artists, and his work adorns everything from furniture to biscuit tins. Margaret's name trips less easily off the tongue, as is often the case for Scotland's brilliant women. But the quality of her work shines through the years. In 2008 her gesso panel *The Red Rose and the White Rose* sold for £1.7 million, setting a world record for a Scottish artwork.

LIVE YOUR LIFE BY MARGARET

While Toshie was clear that Margaret was his collaborator in all things, it is hard for anyone other than the long-departed Mackintoshes to say what was hers and what was his. Perhaps she didn't mind this at the time – after all, they were very much a team. But the world being as it is, Margaret's contribution has been consistently underplayed by comparison to her husband's. He is the famous son of Glasgow celebrated the world over for 'his' buildings, 'his' interiors and 'his' designs; Margaret is mentioned as an afterthought, if at all.

Don't fall into the trap of allowing others to take credit for your work. Partly this is about learning to celebrate your own achievements – not an easy feat for many women, who are too often schooled in being quiet and not 'boasting'. Partly it is about ensuring your name is included in credits, and where there is a question of rights – in artistic work, ideas or designs – make sure you understand what is yours and how to protect it.

When she did get to use it, Margaret's signature was rocking. Develop a good, confident one of your own and sign things with a flourish.

"Could anything be more infantile than a group of grown-up men wasting time, money, and energy on the antics of a fat female crook?"

HARRY PRICE ON
HELEN DUNCAN
1931

HELEN DUNCAN
MEDIUM

H elen MacFarlane was born in the picturesque Perthshire town of Callander in 1897, and from childhood distressed her staunchly Presbyterian parents with a strong interest in the occult. At school she claimed to be clairvoyant, terrifying her fellow pupils with hysterical fits and dire warnings of disaster to come, and earning herself the nickname 'Hellish Nell'.

A supporter of Helen might point out that disaster did indeed follow, as the Great War cut a swathe through her generation. Helen herself married wounded war veteran Henry Duncan, who supported his wife's claim to supernatural talents and encouraged her career as a clairvoyant. By 1926 Helen was actively working as a medium, offering séances in which – for a fee – she would summon the spirits of the recently deceased. She would emit a cloud-like 'ectoplasm' from her mouth, spirits would appear, and witnesses could talk with and even touch their dearly departed.

As Helen's reputation grew she attracted the attention of those investigating the veracity of spiritualists and mediums. In 1928 Harvey Metcalfe used a flash to photograph the 'spirits' in one of her séances. The photographs show a fraud – dolls with masks of papier-mâché or cut from magazines, draped in sheets and other cloths. Based on these emerging doubts, the London Spiritualist Alliance undertook to examine Helen's methods. Analysis of her 'ectoplasm' proved it to contain cheesecloth, egg-white and loo paper; the Alliance committee suspected that Helen swallowed this material before her séances so as to regurgitate it for effect. They asked her to swallow a dye tablet to test this theory. She swallowed the dye, but during the following séance did not produce her 'ectoplasm'. The committee concluded its theory was correct.

Harry Price of the National Laboratory of Psychical Research subsequently paid Helen to perform a set of test séances. During one he requested an X-ray of her, which she refused in fury, attacking Laboratory staff and her husband before running out into the street. She then demanded the X-ray be carried out, leading Price to conclude she had passed the 'ectoplasm' to her husband during the fracas and thus hoped to elude detection. When Price published his report, Helen's former maid Mary McGinlay confessed to having aided Helen with staging, and her husband confessed she did, indeed, regurgitate cheesecloth as 'ectoplasm'. Undaunted, Helen continued to offer séances. In 1933 an attendee in Edinburgh grabbed hold of the 'spirit' of a little girl called Peggy and discovered it to consist of stockinette underwear. The police were called and Helen was convicted for fraudulent mediumship at the Sheriff Court four months later. She was fined £10.

Helen had very publicly been decried as a fraud. So it is particularly bizarre that when she next ended up in the dock, it was to be tried under the Witchcraft Act 1735. It was 1944, Britain was at war and Helen had moved to England to escape her reputation at home. She caught the attention of the English authorities at a séance in Portsmouth, when she claimed the spirit of a sailor had revealed to her that HMS *Barham* had been sunk. It had, but that fact was not public knowledge; only the relatives of casualties had been informed. There were 861 casualties, and so it isn't unthinkable that Helen had simply used gossip to her commercial advantage, but the obsession with secrecy at the time meant anyone leaking sensitive information might soon find themselves under arrest.

Police raided a séance of Helen's and she was arrested. Initially charges of treason were considered, but ultimately she was tried at the Old Bailey for conspiracy to contravene the Witchcraft Act via fraudulent 'spiritual' activity, for obtaining money by false pretences and for public mischief. The Act had not been used for over a century and the case was complicated by the fact that the police raid had yielded no 'ectoplasm' or other physical evidence of fraudulent activity, and most witnesses swore there had been no wrongdoing. Helen offered to demonstrate her powers in court but the judge refused. She was found guilty of contravention of the Act, denied the right of appeal to the House of Lords and imprisoned for nine months in Holloway. Upon hearing her sentence she cried out, 'I have done nothing; is there a God?' Winston Churchill perhaps agreed when he wrote a memo to the Home Secretary about misuse of court resources on 'obsolete tomfoolery'. (Quite comical from a member of the Ancient Order of Druids.) Once released from prison Helen undertook to hold no more séances but almost immediately set up again, being arrested once more in 1956. She died shortly thereafter.

Helen's trial and the scandal surrounding it contributed to the growing support to repeal the Witchcraft Act. This was achieved as a constituent part of the Fraudulent Mediums Act of 1951. Three years later spiritualism was officially recognised as a religion in the UK. Helen retains the dubious honour of being the last person convicted under the Witchcraft Act; despite an ongoing campaign to have her posthumously pardoned, her conviction stands. As Britain's 'Last Witch', a bronze bust of her was commissioned for display in Callander, but complaints from her hometown resulted in its installation in the safer location of Stirling.

LIVE YOUR LIFE BY HELEN

Helen is scarcely a shining example of scrupulous commercial practice, and in some lights she looks like nothing more than a cheap fraud taking advantage of grieving people at their lowest ebb. On the other hand, many established bodies also offer succour to the weary via odd rituals and implausible claims in return for a small charge or donation, and we call that religion. Who knows what Helen believed? Viewed in a kinder light, her act harmed no one beyond divesting them of a few pennies, and perhaps she saw it as a way to give much-needed comfort in a country reeling from the unthinkable loss of life of two World Wars in a space of thirty years.

So think of Helen before you judge anyone too harshly for believing what they believe. By all means challenge behaviour and opinions that are dangerous to yourself or others, but think about how you are most likely to effect a change. Keep it polite and respectful, don't forget to listen and present your challenge constructively and kindly. There's an old saying that you catch more flies with honey than vinegar, and it's true.

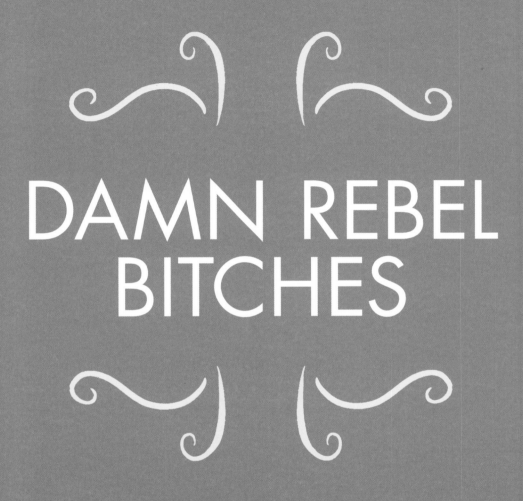

DAMN REBEL
BITCHES

DAMN REBEL BITCHES

The story goes that William Augustus, Duke of Cumberland, once said, 'we must do something about those damn' rebel bitches.'

Normally a man calling women 'bitches' would raise a red flag, but the women of the 1745 Jacobite Rising might have celebrated 'Butcher' Cumberland's frustration with their successes. Despite Cumberland's best efforts to 'pacify' Jacobite territory in the period after the Battle of Culloden – bayonetting wounded soldiers, punishing non-combatants and plundering the Highlands on an epic scale – the women on the Jacobite side weren't for giving up.

Having raised regiments, held the horses and marched with naked blades on their thighs, they turned in the aftermath of the Rising to escapology. Many a fugitive disappeared under the noses of government forces, and more than one axeman was cheated by the actions of a Jacobite wife.

Jacobite rebels of either gender were termed traitors in law but may have rejected the term with the old argument that one cannot be a traitor to a regime one does not recognise as legitimate. This was William Wallace's stance at his trial in 1305, and his period – the Wars of Independence – is another characterised by rebellious females. Like the Jacobite 'bitches', these women were well aware of the price they would pay if caught, and many of them paid it.

It is also worth remembering that many other, forgotten women paid a terrible price for political rebellions in which they were marginally involved, implicated through the actions of others, or indeed in which they were not involved at all. Rebellion throughout Scottish history has tended to result in the brutal dismantling of the sections of society accused of it.

As time moved on, transgressive acts became less dangerous to life and limb, but rebellious women were routinely monstered, ridiculed and mocked for their actions – within the bounds of the law but well outside the accepted standards of the times. What many of these women were doing was something akin to being active citizens, battling for equality and an end to tyranny in various guises. We should perhaps see it as a measure of their effectiveness that they were called unwomanly and improper as a result.

It is worth remembering that the women in the following pages are celebrated primarily because they were unconventional. We might pause to reflect on the quiet voices too, the small actions and the unsung heroines.

Our rebels operated at the edges of society, but the trick is to shift the mainstream, and that is rarely achieved by one or two individuals. Rebels can help fly the flag for progress, but it is truly secured by collective action.

"We celebrate your holy memory today, O right wondrous and glorious Ebba and all those of thy flock who suffered with thee."

MODERN EASTERN ORTHODOX
PRAYER TO EBBA

EBBA OF COLDINGHAM

ABBESS

A house of nuns had been established near Coldingham in the Scottish Borders as early as 660 AD, when the Abbess Saint Ebba the elder accepted her niece, Queen Etheldreda of Northumberland, into the sisterhood there. Poor Etheldreda wanted to be a nun all along but had to endure two marriages first, and the story goes that only one of her husbands respected her desire for chastity. Aunt Ebba's establishment is generally accepted to have stood at St Abb's Head – a name that is thought to commemorate her.

In the 860s another Ebba presided over the nuns at Coldingham, by which time the establishment was the largest in Scotland. But women have rarely been allowed to get on with things in peace, and this younger Abbess Ebba is remembered today for a desperate stand she took to save her own chastity and that of her sisters.

Around 870, a large force of Viking warriors landed on the coast of East Anglia and set about laying waste to the country. Far to the north, Ebba heard word of the approaching hordes and their depredations. The Vikings did not spare priests, monks or nuns and it was surely only a matter of time before they would kill and rape their way towards Ebba and the sisters.

Ebba brought the nuns together and asked them to join her in extreme action to preserve their vows of chastity. She took a razor and attacked her face, cutting open (some sources say off) her nose and lip with the intention of horrifying the invaders at the sight. The nuns followed their Abbess's example.

When the Vikings broke into the convent, they found the nuns mutilated and drenched in blood. Disgusted, they fled. Ebba's desperate order had spared her nuns the horror of rape, but it did not spare their lives. The Vikings set fire to the buildings, and the martyr sisters perished in the flames.

LIVE YOUR LIFE BY EBBA

There is a theory that Ebba's last stand gives rise to the saying, 'cutting off one's nose to spite one's face'. Depressingly, the saying is also linked to the stories of at least four other holy women who are said to have done the same thing, to avoid the same fate.

This fact underlines that, across the world, men have been brutally abusing women for millennia in order to humiliate, terrorise or wipe out populations. Military commanders may encourage soldiers to engage in rape as a reward for victory – in older texts women are covered by the phrase 'spoils of war' – or sexual violence may be deliberately deployed to erode the fabric of a community or to systemically attack its lineage. Victims may be forced into prostitution or sold into slavery, raising funds for ongoing conflict. Sexually transmitted diseases, maternal mortality and increased rates of domestic violence within destabilised communities are all linked to the use of rape as a weapon of war.

Today, international law classifies conflict-related sexual violence as a war crime and a crime against humanity, and it can be considered genocide. It is a feature of many modern conflicts, with devastating consequences for millions of individuals and their communities around the world. One United Nations Peacekeeper has commented, 'It has probably become more dangerous to be a woman than a soldier in armed conflict.'

You can help fight the use of rape as a weapon of war, and help support survivors, by donating or otherwise getting involved with campaigns by charities including Unicef, Amnesty International and others.

"Let her be closely confined in an abode of stone and iron made in the shape of a cross, and let her be hung up out of doors in the open air at Berwick, that both in life and after her death, she may be a spectacle and eternal reproach to travellers."

EDWARD I OF ENGLAND PASSES JUDGEMENT ON
ISABELLA OF BUCHAN
1306

ISABELLA MACDUFF

COUNTESS OF BUCHAN

sabella was the daughter of Donnchadh III, Earl of Fife, and was therefore married off good and young, as was the fate of wealthier young ladies back in the day. Her husband was John, Earl of Buchan, and the marriage was designed to ally the MacDuffs to the Comyns, one of the most powerful families in the war-torn Scotland of the time. Unless you have particular enthusiasm for history – or for *Outlaw King* – you might not have heard of the Comyns but you've almost certainly heard of Robert Bruce, their main rival to the Scottish throne – and the guy with his privates on show in *Outlaw King*.

In 1306, Robert Bruce stuck a knife into the Red Comyn – John III, Lord of Badenoch – at the altar of the Greyfriars Kirk in Dumfries. This was a dark deed even by the low standards of the times and the Earl of Buchan switched his loyalties to Edward I of England in fury. Isabella stuck with blood ties and gave her support instead to her cousin Robert.

When Robert Bruce was crowned King of Scots at Scone in 1306, Isabella defied her husband to fulfil the tradition that a member of the MacDuff clan should place the crown on the new king's head. She was to pay for this decision in full. The Bruce was defeated at the Battle of Methven later that year, and sent Isabella north with his female relatives to safety in Orkney – or so he thought.

Isabella, Elizabeth and Marjorie Bruce rested on their journey at the chapel of St Duthac in Tain. Theoretically, if somewhat hypocritically given Robert the Bruce's altar-front attack on the Red Comyn, they should have been safe within the walls of the church. But the Earl of Ross betrayed them and handed them to the English. Perhaps he consoled himself over his sanctuary breaking with the thought that at least he didn't commit an actual murder on holy ground.

Under Edward I's orders, Isabella was kept in a cage for four years. Accounts vary as to whether this was the open-air hanging hell described in the quote on page 148 and dramatised in various films, or a heavily barred room within Berwick Castle. Either way, it was unlikely to have been an arrangement conducive to Isabella's health. As the Bruce's power grew, the women's value as hostages was reconsidered and Isabella was transferred to the relative safety of a nunnery. Elizabeth and Marjorie Bruce were returned to Scotland in exchange for the release of English noblemen taken prisoner after the Battle of Bannockburn. Of Isabella there is no mention after 1313; it seems likely that she died in captivity.

LIVE YOUR LIFE BY ISABELLA

Isabella is remembered as a lady in an actual, no-shit, metal cage, but cages can take other forms. Have you ever noticed a friend suddenly seem to forget that she ever had any opinions of her own and instead start parroting the thoughts and preferences of a new partner? Have you ever done it yourself? And have you ever thought it has gone too far?

Many of us draw back a bit from friendships and other activities when we first meet a new partner, and enjoy getting to know them and trying out the stuff they like instead. This is quite natural and as a result it can be tough to spot when a new relationship is actually suppressing your own or a friend's personality.

Isabella knew her own mind and took responsibility for her own actions. Make a vow to yourself that you won't ever give up your own personality to fit a new relationship – if you need to do that, the relationship's not a fit, it's a cage. If you see a friend doing it, do your best to make it clear that you're there for her and want to talk whenever she's ready.

You can always speak to the National Domestic Abuse Helpline on 0808 2000 247 for support and advice if you feel your relationship has become controlling or abusive.

"bha sannt aige
air a bhith mòr, nuair
a chuir e bhuaithe
a bhean."

"he was greedy for power, when he
cast off his wife."

DONALD MACINTYRE (SOUTH UIST)
ON JOHN OF ISLAY
1952

AMY NICRUAIRIDH
AMY OF GARMORAN
DISPOSSESSED HEIRESS AND RELIGIOUS PATRON

Amy of Garmoran was born around 1315, and like Devorgilla of Galloway a century earlier, might have gone down in history as one of those females whose story is viewed almost entirely through the lens of the opportunities it brought the men in her life. Like Devorgilla, though, Amy put her fortune to use in building and restoring religious institutions and other buildings across the country, and for this reason she is remembered to the present day.

Amy was a direct descendant of Somerled, a half-Norse, half-Gaelic warlord who seized control of the Kingdom of the Isles in 1148. In the years after Somerled's death his descendants formed three powerful kindreds ruling west coast Scotland. The MacDougalls had their powerbase in Argyll and the MacDonalds in Islay. Amy's branch, the MacRurys, controlled the northernmost islands. Their chief was 'Rí Innse Gall' or 'King of the Hebrides'.

After the MacDougalls opposed the claim of Robert Bruce to the Scottish throne in the early 1300s, their lands in Argyll were further divided between the MacDonalds under Angus Òg of Islay, the MacRurys under Amy's father Ruaidhri Mac Ailein, and other clans. Amy's father was later dispossessed for plotting against the Bruce, but when he died and her brother Raghnall succeeded, the family managed to regain control of the Small Isles, the Outer Hebrides and Garmoran – Moidart, Knoydart, Morar and Ardnamurchan.

Around 1337 the Pope gave a special dispensation to allow Amy to marry her third cousin John, son of Angus Òg of Islay. The couple had three sons

– John, Godfrey and Ranald – and a daughter, Mary. In 1346 Amy's brother Ronald was assassinated and the MacRury lands passed to Amy. Amy and John now controlled most of the West Coast. John began to call himself *Dominus Insularum* – Lord of the Isles. Sadly, Amy didn't last long as his lady.

In 1350 John of Islay divorced Amy to marry Margaret, the daughter of Robert the High Steward of Scotland, heir to the king. The marriage was agreed on condition that Amy's sons would no longer be John's successors.

Tradition says that Amy had given no grounds for divorce and, despite the best efforts of her ex-husband, she retained control of her own lands and supported her sons in their claims to inherit. She is said to have built St Michael's Temple on the island of Grimsay and the monastery and nunneries at Balivanich and Baile nan Cailleach in Benbecula. She restored the Trinity Temple in North Uist, originally built by her great-great-great aunt Beathag, daughter of Somerled. She is also credited with building the tower of Borve Castle in Benbecula and extending the fortress of Castle Tioram in Moidart, which became a stronghold of her son Ranald.

John's sons with Margaret inherited his title and much of his lands, but Ranald successfully petitioned that Garmoran and the North Isles were rightfully his through his mother. His descendants formed Clanranald and the MacDonells of Glengarry. Amy's younger son Godfrey became Lord of Uist.

We do not know the date of Amy's death, but tradition has it that she was buried on Iona, the location of another religious institution founded by her great-great-great aunt Beathag and the traditional burial-place of the Scottish kings. The tradition is testament to her importance in Gaelic society, in her own time and in folk memory that outlasted her by seven hundred years.

LIVE YOUR LIFE BY AMY

Amy's divorce has gone down in history as an extreme case in which one partner was motivated, it seems, by greed for power and influence, and the other was put aside against her will.

Even in more recognisable scenarios, it is often the case that one spouse decides to leave a marriage after thinking about it for many months or even years. Psychologically, that person has already left the marriage. Their spouse, on the other hand, may be completely blindsided by their decision and may still be entirely committed to the marriage.

If you are ever in the scenario in which you wish to leave a marriage, it will help if you can understand where your spouse is in the process. Your spouse may find the situation frightening and distressing and this can result in anger and unreasonable behaviour. You may need to allow your spouse time to come to terms with the idea of the end of the marriage. If you can understand this, you may be able to make the processes easier for both partners.

If you are a blindsided spouse, seek support from friends and loved ones (but not children). Bring a friend you trust to meet your solicitor, at least for the first time. A friend can take in information more easily and can offer you emotional support.

When negotiating the details of a divorce, try to avoid recrimination and discussion of past behaviours, hurt and pain. In Scotland there is no concept of blame in a divorce action. The courts are there to ensure that your property and money are fairly divided and that the welfare of your children is safeguarded.

"De'il gie you colic, the wame o' ye, fause thief!"

JENNY GEDDES
CURSES JAMES HANNAY
1637

JENNY GEDDES
PROTESTER

On Sunday 23 July 1637, James Hannay, Dean of Edinburgh, took the pulpit at St Giles and began to read from the Booke of Common Prayer. He did not get far. Jenny Geddes, a market-trader, stood up, picked up her stool and threw it straight at the Minister's head.

Jenny's action sparked off quite the riot within the walls of St Giles, as Bibles, stools, sticks and stones rained down on Hannay. Eventually the protesters were expelled from the church by officers of the law, although they remained outside for the rest of Hannay's service, hammering on the doors and throwing missiles at the windows. The mob gathered – imagine Edinburgh at closing time on a rugby weekend, multiply the drunkenness and violence quotients by at least four and you'll have an idea of what that meant – and soon the Provost and magistrates were trapped in the City Chambers.

The whole stooshie was provoked by Hannay's use of the Booke of Common Prayer. The Booke was the work of a commission set up by King Charles I, with the stated aim of providing a prayer book suitable for Scotland. The real objective was to encourage Scotland to use Anglican-style church services instead of the more Puritan services preferred north of the Border. It was a wildly unpopular move.

The protests in Edinburgh set off rioting in other cities and Lord Advocate Thomas Hope began negotiations with the Privy Council for the withdrawal of the Booke in the hope of calming the storm. King Charles turned these demands down. Across Scotland, believers signed the National Covenant, recording their opposition to the introduction of measures such as the Booke without the agreement of Parliament and the General Assembly of the Church of Scotland. The Church expelled its Bishops and Archbishops and became a Presbyterian institution.

Uneasy relations between Scotland and England boiled over into the Bishops' Wars, the beginning of the Wars of the Three Kingdoms. Eventually the English Civil War would see Charles I lose his head.

Nothing is known of Jenny Geddes beyond this story, and some people doubt that she ever existed. Others have chosen to commemorate her. There is a sculpture of a three-legged creepie called the 'Cutty Stool' in St Giles in her memory, and Robert Burns named his faithful mare Jenny Geddes.

LIVE YOUR LIFE BY JENNY

If you feel passionately about an issue, why not get involved? Throwing furniture at people isn't generally advised, but the CORE principle – Campaign, Organise, Recruit, Educate – is a good place to start. It's especially important that women raise their voices to discuss the issues that concern them. Women are still routinely under-represented in politics, making up around one fifth of elected politicians in parliaments across the globe, and studies show that without women's input, issues that disproportionately affect them are routinely ignored.

There are many ways to become more active. You can contact your local elected representative to raise issues, share campaigns online or join and support a political party or campaign group. If you prefer, you can make a difference at a local level by joining community boards and groups, from PTAs at school to management committees of community centres or other facilities. Helping out within these structures can help you develop great skills and you can often meet people from across the generations with whom you share views and interests and from whom you can learn an immense amount.

"If I meet my dear lord well, and am so happy as to be able to serve him, I shall think all my trouble well re-paid. "

WINIFRED MAXWELL
WRITES TO HER SISTER-IN-LAW MARY
CHRISTMAS DAY 1716

WINIFRED MAXWELL OF NITHSDALE

COUNTESS

Winifred Herbert's early life was one plot after another. She was born around 1678 to William Herbert, Earl of Powis and his wife Elizabeth Somerset, two years after William had been carted off to the Tower of London, accused of taking part in a conspiracy to kill King Charles II. This 'Popish Plot' was a fabrication by the rather woefully named Titus Oates and Israel Tonge. You may speculate in your own time as to whether Oates and Tonge would have been more contented souls had their parents been kinder to them in the naming department.

William Herbert remained in the Tower for six long years. Elizabeth's attempts to free him endangered her, too, particularly when she became implicated in the 'Meal-tub Plot', which is the last false plot you need to concern yourself with in this story but it's too well named to leave out. The Tower of London will come up again . . .

When William was finally released in 1684 – the dates imply that Winifred was conceived on a conjugal visit – the Herberts enjoyed four short years of relative peace until the Glorious Revolution of 1688, when King James II was deposed in favour of his Protestant son-in-law William of Orange. William Herbert spirited James's wife Queen Mary and their infant son James, Prince of Wales, out of England to safety in France. King James rewarded him with the title Marquess of Powis. The new establishment at home in England rewarded him with permanent exile and the loss of his titles and estates.

King James built a court around himself in France and the Herberts took their place as advisors and confidantes. Winifred grew up in this Jacobite world – Jacobite means supporter of James – and met her future husband, William Maxwell, 5th Earl of Nithsdale, when he came to pay his respects to the exiled king. The couple married in 1699 and Winifred became a countess, returning to live on her husband's estates in Dumfriesshire.

In 1715 William Maxwell joined a Jacobite Rising seeking to restore James Francis Edward Stuart to the throne – that baby Winifred's father had spirited out of England in 1688. William was captured at the Battle of Preston and, like his father-in-law before him, was imprisoned in the Tower. Convicted as a traitor, he was sentenced to death. Winifred immediately left for London, making much of the month-long journey by horse in bitter December snows. Supported by friends, she determined to make a personal appeal to King George I, but the king would not hear her. William wrote his 'dying speech' and a letter to his family, and prepared to meet his end.

On the eve of William's execution, Winifred secured permission to visit him to bid farewell. She arrived with her maid and two female friends. They distributed drinking money among the guards and proceeded to enter the cell one-by-one to say their tearful farewells. At last it was Winifred's turn. Fretting aloud about her maid wandering off, she entered the cell and was heard to converse with her husband for the last time. She latched the door behind her as she left, telling the guards that her husband was saying his prayers, but that she was convinced she would still secure the petition she needed to halt the execution.

When the guards next entered William's cell, they found it empty. The Earl had made his escape long since, disguised in extra layers of clothing Winifred's retinue had worn. With rouge on his cheeks, a wig on his head, a large cloak around him and his face buried in his handkerchief, 'Mrs Mills' had fled with Winifred's women while Winifred carried on a two-sided conversation with herself in the cell. William was the last person ever to escape the Tower.

The couple hid in London until William could be smuggled to France. Winifred made a risky return journey to Scotland to settle affairs and then made her way to join him, evading detection by government forces out looking hard for the escapee Earl. She rejoined William at the Jacobite court and they lived out their lives with the king-in-exile in Rome. William did little to indicate that he had been worth the extreme effort his wife had gone to, but Winifred became governess to King James's son Charles – Bonnie Prince Charlie – and in this way supported her husband and their own children.

LIVE YOUR LIFE BY WINIFRED

Winifred is a totally brilliant example of a woman keeping her cool under pressure. The plan as she rode to London was to petition the king for William's release. That didn't work, and so the plot to spring him from the Tower was adopted instead. This required Winifred to gain the trust of the guards, distract, confuse and befuddle them, orchestrate exchanges of clothing and disguises, impersonate her husband and lastly walk out of the Tower as if butter wouldn't melt in her mouth. All this while placing herself and her friends in significant danger.

While it's not likely you'll be trying to spring anyone from prison any time soon, learning to keep calm under pressure can help you in a range of situations, from public speaking to challenging driving conditions, difficult negotiations to tight deadlines.

Understanding what happens in your body when you panic is a useful first step. When it registers a threat, your brain releases hormones that flood your system and result in a 'fight or flight' response, with shallow breathing, narrowed vision and muscles pumped with blood. This might be helpful if you were a zebra and with a lion after you; in the modern (human) world it helps us freeze, palpitate and generally not cope well with whatever situation is facing us.

Neuroscientists now believe that understanding and naming emotions can help counteract the effects of fight or flight. It can be helpful to articulate to yourself that you are panicking – which doesn't mean in any way that you're actually in any danger – and you may be able to stop your brain's response. Breathe slowly and deeply to counteract the physiological effects, bringing oxygen back into your lungs and bloodstream.

Now try relabelling your emotions. *Fear* might better be called *excitement*; *apprehension* could be called *anticipation*. By owning and reframing your responses, you can learn to use these to your advantage – be *poised in readiness* as opposed to *frozen in fear*.

FIONNGHAL NIC DHÒMHNAILL
FLORA MACDONALD
TACKSMAN'S DAUGHTER

The heroine of many a biscuit tin and a song learned by almost every Scottish child ever to attend primary school, Flora MacDonald was born in 1722 in Milton in South Uist to Ranald and Marion MacDonald. Her father was a tacksman, a member of the minor gentry, but he died when she was two. Her mother married again, to a Skyeman, and Flora was brought up under the supervision of her father's cousin MacDonald of Sleat.

In 1746, the Jacobite Rising of Charles Edward Stuart – 'Bonnie Prince Charlie' – lay in ruins. Thousands of Jacobites had fallen at the Battle of Culloden, and government troops were hunting survivors throughout the length and breadth of the Highlands. There was a price of £30,000 on the head of the Prince. He hoped to escape to France, but in order to do so he would have to evade hundreds of soldiers scouring the west coast and the islands, and the Royal Navy, patrolling the seas.

Flora was in Uist when a tall young fugitive with a bit of an accent arrived in the area. He had been living rough and was showing the effects of weeks in the heather. Flora agreed to transport him to Skye, dressed in women's clothing. She called him Betty Burke, her maid, and procured permission to allow her to travel to the mainland with a crew of six men and two personal servants. One of these was 'Betty'.

Flora and 'Betty' – aka Charles – made their way from Uist across the Minch to Skye, where they spent a night in the house of MacDonald of Kingsburgh in the north of the island. Charles escaped, finally to be taken off to France by ship

"a name that
will be mentioned in
history, and if courage
and fidelity be virtues,
mentioned with
honour."

DR SAMUEL JOHNSON ON FLORA MACDONALD
A JOURNEY TO THE WESTERN ISLES OF SCOTLAND
1775

from Lochaber. Flora was arrested by the government. In Applecross Bay on 12 July 1746, she gave a statement detailing the events of the preceding days.

Flora spent a year in captivity, taken south to the Tower of London. Jacobite prisoners were not treated well in government captivity in general, but Flora's family were able to arrange for her to live outside the Tower under effective house-arrest. In 1747 she was released under the Act of Indemnity, and returned home to Skye. She married Allan MacDonald, the son of MacDonald of Kingsburgh, and the couple inherited the Kingsburgh estate. In the 1770s they emigrated to North Carolina, joining the government side in the War of Independence. They lost two of their sons and their American holdings and returned home to live out their days in Skye.

Before her return to Scotland, Flora was asked by Frederick, Prince of Wales, the son of George II, why she had helped the Prince although her family were not Jacobites. Flora said that she had done it out of charity, and that she would have done the same for Frederick had he been in distress.

LIVE YOUR LIFE BY FLORA

Flora's life is a lesson in image management. She was by all accounts small and delicate, and used these qualities to her advantage – few other prisoners of the Jacobite era gained the right to house arrest or audiences with royalty. She embraced the romantic portrayal of her created by others, posing for portraits with a Jacobite rose despite her family's Hanoverian sympathies, and complying with requests from those who wished to meet a Jacobite heroine. She even charmed Samuel Johnson, who expected to meet a 'barbarous people' on his tour of the Western Isles.

So, what can we take from Flora's decision to work with her own legend? Perhaps the thought that our true selves are ultimately private, and we may keep them that way if we so desire. Flora was certainly kind – she risked her life and freedom to help a man she did not know – and her story grew into a romantic one, but the experiences she survived and determination she exhibited speak to a core of steel. She showed that core when it suited her, and didn't when it didn't; the very definition of a self-possessed woman we can seriously admire.

ELIZABETH GRANT

SEAMSTRESS

The histories of the women of the 1745 Jacobite Rising – and their Hanoverian counterparts – give a glimpse into the lives of working women as well as the exploits of countesses and clan chiefs' daughters. One sterling example is Elizabeth Grant of Banff, who is listed as having made her living by her needle.

Elizabeth's tale is preserved in documents pertaining to her imprisonment in York and subsequent sentence of transportation. She was most probably captured with sixty-three (male) 'Highland rebels' and nine 'Highland women' handed over by the Duke of Cumberland to the keeper of Appleby Jail after a skirmish at Clifton Moor near Penrith.

If Elizabeth was indeed part of this group, she and her fellow prisoners were marched through the winter snows for some two weeks until they reached York, where the intention was to imprison them in the Castle. Thomas Herring, Archbishop of York, saw the prisoners arrive in the city and commented on the poor state of them – many were barefoot and clothed in rags. Later accounts of the group of prisoners to which Elizabeth belonged in York detail only eight women. Perhaps one perished in the cold or escaped in transit.

Elizabeth and the other women were held in a cell in the County Prison in newer accommodation than was available in the Castle. Evidently they were able to mix with their male counterparts, however, because Elizabeth managed to marry one Edmund Clavering, a Jacobite who had been captured after a skirmish at Lowther Hall.

"taken in actual rebellion."

ELIZABETH GRANT'S RECORD
YORK PRISON
1745

The marriage was solemnised by Father John Rivett, a Catholic priest who was also imprisoned in the Castle, and it was strictly against the rules. When he was interrogated, Father Rivett claimed he had married them 'to prevent sin', implying that they were lovers already.

Elizabeth and Edmund's wedding present from the authorities was not very jolly; on 8 November 1746 Edmund was one of eleven Jacobite prisoners hanged at York.

Elizabeth spent another five months in prison before she and six other women were sent to Liverpool for transportation to Antigua as indentured servants. In May the transport ship *The Veteran* set sail with Elizabeth on board. Just off Antigua it was attacked by a French privateer, captured and taken to Martinique. The Jacobite prisoners were released from their sentences by the French authorities and offered the opportunity to remain in Martinique and make a life there, or to travel to France instead. There is no record of Elizabeth beyond this point.

LIVE YOUR LIFE BY ELIZABETH

The scant records of Elizabeth's life are suggestive of a personality able to make the best of any situation. Things will on occasion go pear-shaped for all of us, and so it's worth learning how to cope.

First off, try to put things in perspective. Will this matter in a year's time? In most situations, the answer will be no. Next, take a deep breath and work on accepting things as they are. Have you missed an onward travel connection? Is the curry really ruined? Are you stuck in your old job or jobless for a while longer?

Once you accept the situation, you can start to work out a plan of action to move forward. Rebook your travel, give up on the curry as a bad job and make a sandwich, start the job search anew. Part of acceptance is giving up on the recriminations. Okay, you may wish to work out the take-aways – that way, you can do things differently next time – but this should be a quick process. You definitely don't need to beat yourself up about things. This has no positive impact at all – there are far better things to do with your time. Funnily enough, the old Scottish fatalism can come in handy here – that saying beloved of grannies, 'what's for ye will no go by ye', can remind you to keep looking forward.

Also: listen to *Lemonade*. We call all benefit from the glory that is Beyoncé.

CHRISTIAN SUTHERLAND

LADY REAY

NOBLEWOMAN

Balnakeil House in Durness was famous for the merry-making of the MacKay family, who hawked, hunted, fished, shot, feasted and danced there in the finest aristocratic Gaelic tradition. MacKay chief Lord Reay kept a piper, a harpist and a jester, and when one visitor left Balnakeil in 1669 he took with him gifts of guns, longbows, an antique sword, a pair of deerhounds, a suit of silk and a Shetland pony. It gives the gift-bags at the Oscars a run for their money, for all their big-game safaris and vibrators.*

The women of the MacKay family seem to have been as fabulous as their hospitality. Among the best remembered are Barbara, who sprung her husband from captivity after an audience with Oliver Cromwell in 1649, and Christian, who pulled off a daring escape mission of her own around 1748.

Born around 1725 to James Sutherland of Pronsy and his wife Margaret, Christian became the second wife of Donald, 4th Lord Reay in 1741. The MacKays were loyal Hanoverians in the '45 Rising and safe from reprisals, but life was still characterised by a heavy army presence. Conditions in the army itself were difficult, and many men were pressed into service. At some time in 1748, Christian was at home in Balnakeil when an army deserter named Kenneth Sutherland bolted into the house and up the stairs. The young man was clearly terrified; a quick glance from the window showed Christian that a troop of redcoats was hot on his heels.

allegedly

"Cha b' aithne dhomhs' am *pass*,
An deach e às, ged bhi'dh e marbh;
Ach eadar chasan boireannaich,
Gun bhoneid 's e gun arm;
Glè fhaisg don alt an d' rugadh e
Siud thugadh e air falbh!"

"I can't say which pass
He went out by, for his life;
But between a woman's legs
Without bonnet or weapons;
Very near the route he was born,
He made his escape!"

ROB DONN MACAOIDH
ON CHRISTIAN SUTHERLAND'S EXPLOITS
PRAISE POEM COMPOSED c.1748

Christian immediately bundled Kenneth into a tiny cupboard on the first-floor landing of her house and gathered her nerves. Instructing her servants to admit the soldiers, she escorted them into the living quarters and offered them the famous MacKay hospitality. Refreshments were brought and soon a party was underway, with much merriment and dancing.

Ladies' skirts at the time were so wide that two women could struggle to pass one another on a narrow street. Lady Reay sent one of her women to conceal the deserter under her skirts. Once he was crouched down and the fabric arranged, all she had to do was walk slowly past the oblivious redcoats and out of the house. The deserter was safe.

LIVE YOUR LIFE BY CHRISTIAN

A number of fashion 'rules' prescribed to women effectively translate as instructions for how to disappear. These rules teach that the aim is to make yourself look smaller, to fade into the background, or to accept that after a certain age you should no longer be seen in 'inappropriate' attire – or perhaps be seen at all. In Christian's era the aim was quite the opposite – women showed their status through colour, pattern and texture, and the aim was to take up as much space as you could. In the MacKay house, this fact saved a man's life.

Channel Christian and refuse to fade into the background – experiment instead with the many ways clothes can bring you joy. Read up on Iris Apfel, follow Amber Butchart, browse the street style snaps from Fashion Weeks around the world or develop a love for Marimekko. Try an experimental silhouette. Wear something bright with something else bright. Be seen. Have fun.

"He could not be in better security, or more honourably treated."

CHARLES EDWARD STUART
HANDS ANGUS MACKINTOSH INTO THE CUSTODY OF HIS WIFE
1746

ANNE FARQUHARSON
LADY MACKINTOSH
REBEL

Anne Farquharson of Invercauld was born into a staunchly Jacobite family in 1723 and married Angus Mackintosh, chief of the Clan Mackintosh. Early in 1744 her husband was offered the chance to captain one of three new Independent Companies being raised by the Earl of Loudoun to support the government. Anne dressed herself in male attire – the Jacobite penchant for dressing in the clothes of the opposite sex went both ways – and rode around the glens enlisting men. Soon she had the complement required for her husband to take up his place as captain. The company fought as part of the Black Watch in the Jacobite Rising of 1745.

Once the Rising was underway, Anne switched sides, presumably donned her breeks again and raised between two hundred and four hundred men from among the Mackintoshes and Clan Chattan to fight for the Prince. She became known as 'Colonel Anne', although women couldn't command in the field and Anne's regiment was therefore commanded by the chief of the MacGillivrays.

A month after Anne's regiment joined the Prince's Army, the Prince was staying with Anne at Moy Hall when a young messenger came to say that 1,500 of the Earl of Loudon's men planned to raid Moy to capture the Prince and claim the £30,000 reward on his head. Among this force were Anne's own husband's men.

There is no evidence as to who sent the messenger, fifteen-year-old Lachlan Macintosh, but a prime suspect is Lady Drummuir, who lived in one of the most desirable houses in Inverness and put up both Prince Charles and the Duke of Cumberland during the course of the Rising.

Lachlan came to Moy at five in the morning. Anne was still in her nightie, and she had almost no men with her to mount a defence. Relying instead on her wits, she sent the local blacksmith Donald Fraser and four other men to hide by the road with instructions to fire on the raiding force and generate enough noise and battle cries to make the government forces think they were about to walk into an ambush by the Jacobite army. The ploy worked. Donald Fraser killed the MacLeod piper Dòmhnall Bàn MacCrimmon – being a musician has always been a tough gig – the others cried 'Advance, Keppoch' and 'Clanranald! Charge!' and the government forces fled.

A month later, Anne's husband was captured north of Inverness by the Jacobites, with around three hundred of Loudon's men. The Prince handed Mackintosh into his wife's care. The story goes that she greeted him with the words, 'Your servant, Captain,' to which he replied, 'Your servant, Colonel.'

When the Jacobite army was defeated at Culloden, Anne was arrested and turned over into the care of her mother-in-law. Many years later she met Prince William, Duke of Cumberland in London where she was attending an event with her husband. The Duke asked her to dance to a pro-government melody. She returned the compliment, asking him to dance to a Jacobite tune.

LIVE YOUR LIFE BY ANNE

Colonel Anne reminds us that women have been playing their part in major events since long before they had the right to vote, the chance to fight in wars if they chose (being victims of said wars was of course always on the cards), to control their own property or to operate as independent beings in general. Remember Anne by exercising those rights that women of her era didn't have, and which we enjoy today thanks to the efforts of other women between then and now.

Most pressingly, don't take your vote for granted. Remember that in a significant percentage of UK elections, 'didn't vote' would actually have won if it were a position. Turn up and take your part in democracy. You can even wear trousers to mark the occasion!

"Until women assume the place in society which good sense and good feeling alike assign to them, human improvement must advance but feebly. It is in vain that we would circumscribe the power of one half of our race, and that by far the most important and influential."

FANNY WRIGHT
COURSE OF POPULAR LECTURES
1829

FANNY WRIGHT
LECTURER, WRITER AND FREETHINKER

From mother-in-law jokes to 'anti-nag gags', so-called humour has long gone hand-in-hand with misogyny. Back in the 1820s a side-splitting cartoon showed Fanny Wright as a goose in a dress, a 'down(w)right gabbler'. Fanny had dared speak her mind in an era when women were supposed to remain at home with their mouths shut, and the cartoonists saw their chance. How those 19th-century gents must have LOLed.

Frances Wright was born in Dundee in 1795. Her parents were radicals, involved in a network of major thinkers and revolutionaries, but both died young, leaving Fanny an orphan at the age of two. She and her sister Camilla were brought up by her mother's sister in England – their brother was sent to another branch of the family – and returned north when Fanny was sixteen to live with an uncle who was Professor of Moral Philosophy at Glasgow University. By this time Fanny was already a precocious thinker, and by the age of eighteen she had written her first book.

In 1818, Fanny travelled to America with Camilla, spending two years touring the country before returning home. During this time she developed her strong beliefs in equality and in feminism. She saw particular dangers in organised religion, in marriage and in capitalism. She campaigned for free education, the emancipation of slaves and for sexual freedom for women, including access to birth control. She wrote on these subjects in a range of books, in the *Free Inquirer* newspaper, which she co-founded, and in *The Sentinel*, which she edited. Her writing led to the first of many return trips to America, where she became known as a social reformer, spending time with the Utopian thinker Robert Owen, who had moved on from New Lanark to Indiana. While living in Owen's community, she determined to found her own Utopian commune.

Fanny's settlement at Nashoba in Tennessee was intended to demonstrate a model of a working farm where slaves could earn their own freedom through labour while receiving education. To a modern eye, this well-intended proposition raises some questions, but Nashoba had other issues too. The land was infested with mosquitos and malaria was rife, and its yield was low. When Fanny left for a time due to illness, her managers instituted a system of harsh punishments for black workers, and relationships between white staff and black women caused a scandal in the local area. By 1828, the project's finances were in ruin, and by 1830 it was over. Fanny chartered a ship to take the workers to Haiti, where they could live as free people.

Fanny returned from the Haiti voyage pregnant and went to France, where she married a French doctor and gave birth to daughter Silva. A second child was born to the couple but died in infancy, and so Silva was given her birthdate in order to regularise her birth.

Fanny continued to lecture and write on the emancipation of slaves and the rights of working people. She also promoted women's rights, assistance for those in need, and the paramount important of education. Silva looked after her in later years, until her death in 1851. It is a sobering thought that 110 years were to pass before birth control was normalised for women in Britain via the pill, and another 116 until unmarried women could legally access it.

LIVE YOUR LIFE BY FANNY

Fanny was one of life's triers, understanding that it's better to fail than never to give it a shot. She was so far ahead of her time that many of her ideas had no chance, but she kept on banging the drum for the things she believed in nonetheless. Depressingly, she faced vitriol as much from other women as from men. Catherine Beecher, an American campaigner for education and women's rights, had some particularly bitchy comments to pass on Fanny's public lecturing:

'There she stands, with brazen front and brawny arms, attacking the safeguards of all that is venerable and sacred in religion, all that is safe and wise in law, all that is pure and lovely in domestic virtue.'

That's right – Catherine thought it worth passing a comment about the size of Fanny's arms in order to shut her down. No matter how strong your belief in the sisterhood, it's enough to give you pause.

Theorists posit that women keeping other women down is a function of inequality. One explanation goes that women are beaten down until they come to believe that any gains they have made personally are threatened by other women. Men essentially have it all, they accept, and there's a small bit left for women, which has to be fought over with other women. Other theories include the idea that women wish to distance themselves from other women in order to avoid discrimination – subconsciously they understand that their workplace values 'male' behaviour over 'female' and so they wish to distance and distinguish themselves from other women.

This all sounds very plausible, although it also sounds plausible that women are individuals and some of them are unpleasant individuals or indeed downright twisted. We all know at least one and the issues with having them in the sisterhood are an extension of the basic sadness that they're part of the human race.

Either way, the system needs to change, and our understanding of what women bring – and why it doesn't have to look exactly like what men bring – needs to develop. You can get involved with supporting this work for future generations via initiatives such as *Girl Up*.

"The females in this city who have much leisure for philanthropic objects are I believe very numerous but unhappily that is not the class who take an active part in the cause here neither the noble, the rich, nor the learned are to be found advocating our cause. Our subscribers and most efficient members are all in the middling and working classes."

JANE SMEAL
WRITES TO ELIZABETH PEASE
1836

JANE SMEAL
AND
ELIZA WIGHAM
ACTIVISTS

n the 1700s and 1800s, Glasgow formed one point on a shameful triangle of trade. British goods sailed down the Clyde, bound for Africa, where they were exchanged for slaves. The ships sailed onward to the New World and unloaded their human cargo, filling the empty holds with slave-produced sugar, rum and tobacco bound for sale back home. Once this awful triangle was complete, it began all over again.

In the hundreds of years that it lasted, the Atlantic slave trade sustained enormous profits for white planters at the cost of the freedom of as many as ten million people, countless thousands of whom died in stifling ship-holds, through disease and malnutrition and under appalling treatment at the hands of slave masters and colonial authorities. Much of the money that built Glasgow's great civic buildings and 'tobacco mansions' – and contributed to Scotland's wider wealth – was the result of this trade. The street names remind us – Buchanan, Glassford, Ingram, Oswald, Dunlop, Cochrane and many more were 'Tobacco Lords', their fortunes drenched in the blood of their slaves.

Jane Smeal was born in Glasgow in 1801, to a Quaker family. The Quakers were staunchly anti-slavery and believed in women's right to participate in campaigning activity. Jane and her brother William became active in Emancipation activity in Glasgow in the 1820s – Jane as leader and secretary of the Glasgow Ladies' Emancipation Society, and William as the founder of the Glasgow Anti-Slavery Society. They distributed pamphlets, organised boycotts of slave-produced goods and organised meetings, rallies and petitions calling for change.

With her friend Elizabeth Pease, Jane exhorted British women to organise themselves in *Address to the Women of Great Britain*. She was then involved in a Scottish address to the young Queen Victoria that is credited, along with other companion pieces, with helping bring the UK's involvement in the Caribbean slave trade to an end. Even after British-owned slaves were emancipated, America continued to resist abolition, and so Jane's work continued.

In 1840 Jane married John Wigham, a Quaker widower living in Edinburgh with his three surviving children. Of these, twenty-year-old Eliza Wigham was also a passionate abolitionist, attending the World Anti-Slavery Convention in 1840. This was a tremendously important event for the women's suffrage movement as women's dedication to action in the abolition movement on both sides of the Atlantic collided head-on with male determination to silence them. After Eliza's return she and Jane set up a chapter of the Women's Suffrage Society in Edinburgh and began to campaign for votes for women. Other prominent members of the Society were Priscilla Bright McLaren, their president; Elizabeth Pease Nichol, treasurer; and Agnes McLaren, Priscilla's daughter, joint secretary. The group supported the American reformer William Lloyd Garrison's views – he believed, as they did, that women's suffrage was key to social reform, including the ending of slavery.

Jane died in 1888 and Eliza in 1899. Neither saw women gain the vote, but in addition to seeing the end of slavery, they did see women's action address the issue of domestic violence encouraged by alcohol abuse, and end the victimisation of women suspected of prostitution under the Contagious Diseases Act, which Eliza in particular campaigned against ahead of its repeal in 1868.

LIVE YOUR LIFE BY JANE AND ELIZA

There's something very heartwarming in the stepmother-stepdaughter dynamic Jane and Eliza had going. A stepparent-stepchild relationship is not always an easy one to establish, but the Wighams are evidence that it can be really rewarding for both parties.

When you first meet a new partner's child, consider yourself first and foremost another caring adult in the young person's life. Don't rush attempts to form a closer bond – relationships need time to grow. If kids have lost a parent or been through a parental break-up, they may have a particular need to process events and work through their feelings. Support them by always being respectful when it comes to their birth parent, whether the individual is deceased, estranged or part of the child's life – and even if the child is critical of them to you. Allow them one-to-one time with your partner if they need it.

Build the relationship by finding common ground and doing things together that you all genuinely enjoy, from board-game nights to days out. Children are individuals; get to know them on that basis and you'll find the dynamic that works for your new family.

"We ride into a district, introduce ourselves to the police, and tell them we are going to hold a meeting in the village square. Then we get on a chair or a box, as the case may be, form our cycles into a group around it, and deliver the gospel of votes to women."

FLORA DRUMMOND
THE PALL MALL GAZETTE
1907

FLORA DRUMMOND
SUFFRAGETTE

Flora Gibson was born in Manchester in 1878 to tailor Francis Gibson and Sarah Cook. After Flora's birth Francis and Sarah moved back to Sarah's home village of Pirnmill on the Isle of Arran where Flora attended high school on the island before moving to Glasgow to study business and economics. Her ambition was to become a post-mistress but although she passed the necessary qualifications, she was barred from taking up post. The Post Office had just introduced a minimum height requirement of 5 foot 2, and Flora was an inch too short. The injustice rankled and perhaps first brought to Flora's attention the unfair disadvantages facing women wishing to make their way in the world.

Flora's subsequent life recalls Shakespeare's famous line, 'Though she be but little, she is fierce.' She married upholsterer Joseph Drummond and the couple eked out a living in Flora's birthplace of Manchester. Flora was appalled by the situation of the people around her and of women in particular, whose wages were so poor that some turned to prostitution to support their families. Flora became involved in the Independent Labour Party and the Fabian Society, and in 1905 began informally to recruit women from across Lancashire to the Suffragette organisation the Woman's Social and Political Union (WSPU).

In 1906 Flora attended a rally in Manchester to celebrate the release of Suffragettes Christabel Pankhurst and Annie Kenney from prison, where they had been sent for disrupting a Liberal Party meeting by shouting demands for votes for women at speakers including Winston Churchill. Flora had witnessed the arrests and was persuaded to become a full-time organiser of the WSPU. She and Joseph relocated to London and Flora moved into an office in WSPU Headquarters at Clement's Inn.

One of Flora's initiatives was to captain the WSPU Cycling Scouts, formed in 1907 as a means of spreading the word to areas beyond the cities. Each Saturday up to thirty of Flora's Scouts would dress in the Suffragette colours of purple, white, and green, decorate their bikes and pedal off to spread the word.

From her earliest days in London, Flora was also involved in militant action and would go on to be imprisoned nine times as a result. Her headline-grabbing actions included an escapade in which she slipped inside Number 10 Downing Street while her fellow Suffragette Irene Miller created a distraction at the door and another in 1908, when she approached the Houses of Parliament by water, haranguing Members on the terraces overlooking the Thames from the roof of a barge. Later the same year she was one of the organisers of the Trafalgar Square rally, for which she, Christabel and Emmeline Pankhurst were imprisoned in Holloway Prison for inciting attendees to storm the Commons.

Flora did not serve her full sentence on this occasion because she was in the early stages of pregnancy. After the birth of her son – named Keir for Scottish Labour Party founder James Keir Hardie – she and her husband parted company and Flora threw herself back into action. She moved to Glasgow and organised action in Scotland. Edinburgh's women had been slow to mobilise and Flora arranged the city's first march as a response to direct criticism in the Women's Social and Political Union newsletter *Votes for Women*. The theme was 'Have done and can do and will do', and women dressed as Scottish historical figures or in working clothes, carried banners and played the bagpipes. The march was deemed a success, with tens of thousands participating or watching from the pavements of the capital.

Flora earned the nickname The General for leading marches on horseback in military-style dress, with an officer's cap and epaulettes. This marked her out in comparison to many Suffragettes, who strived to present a feminine image in response to campaigns to ridicule them as masculine and unwomanly.

Flora, Annie Kenney and other WSPU representatives met with David Lloyd George and Sir Edward Grey in 1913, when Flora's experiences as one of the few working class Suffragettes informed their approach. Working class women endured terrible pay and conditions, they told Lloyd George, and had not even the recourse men had to representation within parliament. As a result they had no means to challenge their situation in a democratic manner.

Flora also besieged the homes of Ulster MPs Lord Carson and Lord Landsdowne in 1914, with Norah Dacre Fox. Carson and Landsdowne were inciting militancy in Ulster against the Home Rule Bill for Ireland; in interviews Flora and Norah declared that they wished to take refuge with Carson and Landsdowne because they were also inciting militancy but attracting considerably more censure from the authorities for doing so. Both Flora and Norah were sent to Holloway Prison for these actions, where they went on hunger and thirst strike and were subject to the brutal process of force-feeding before being released under the Cat and Mouse Act to recover.

The outbreak of war temporarily resulted in a stand-down by the suffragettes, who determined to support the war effort and took up a populist, jingoistic position. In 1918 the Representation of the People Act gave the vote to women over the age of thirty who owned sufficient property to qualify within the terms of the Act, and in 1928 the Representation of the People Act (Equal Franchise) gave the vote to all women over twenty-one – electoral equality with men.

LIVE YOUR LIFE BY FLORA

Flora understood the power of a costume, and you can tap into it too. Your fashion choices can help you achieve your aspirations, advertise yourself and project your personality. Think Flora, think Frida Kahlo, think Jean Muir, think Coco Chanel. These women had a signature style, and it became a part of them. And just because you they had a formula they knew they could rely on didn't mean they always looked the same. They knew how to play with variations and accessories, or used their signature as an outfit to fall back on when they had 'nothing to wear'.

If the idea of a signature style is tending towards a uniform in your eyes and bringing you out in a sweat remembering school, don't worry; the point is always to be an individual. For you the answer might be choosing to wear whatever you really love and what makes you feel like the best version of you. And if that's a onesie, that's fine too. You do you.

MARY REID MACARTHUR

SUFFRAGIST AND TRADE UNIONIST

Mary Reid Macarthur was born in Glasgow in 1880 and grew up in a middle-class, Conservative-voting family. She attended Glasgow Girls' High School, where she edited the school magazine and conceived of the ambition to become a full-time writer.

After a period studying overseas, Mary began to work for her father as a bookkeeper in his drapery business and to experiment with journalism on the side. In 1902 her father sent her to observe a meeting of the Shop Assistants' Union in Ayr, where a speech by trade unionist John Turner about the abuse of workers by their employers converted her to the cause. Within months Mary had become the secretary of the Ayr branch of the Shop Assistants' Union, where she realised that women's labour conditions were even worse than men's. At this time she met and fell in love with journalist and Independent Labour Party activist Will (W.C.) Anderson, but her mind was firmly on her mission. Her friend Margaret Bondfield suggested that Mary – whom she described as a 'person of genius' – should attend the union's national conference. Mary did, and was elected to the national executive.

Mary had found her calling, and in 1903 she turned down a proposal of marriage from Will and instead moved to London where she became Secretary of the Women's Trade Union League. She was a suffragist – campaigning for votes for all through democratic means as opposed to militant action and civil disobedience – and opposed the position of the Women's Social and Political

Union and the National Union of Women's Suffrage Societies, who were willing to accept a limited extension of the vote to particular groups of women. Mary saw that this approach would seriously limit the number of working women who would become eligible – to perhaps as few as 5 per cent – and believed that it might more generally disadvantage the working classes and stand in the way of extending the vote to the whole adult population.

Mary went on to bring attention to the dreadful sweatshop conditions that were rife in Britain at the time through the Exhibition of Sweated Industries in 1905, and she founded the Anti-Sweating League in 1906. She then founded the National Federation of Women Workers (NFWW) to give women a dedicated voice in trade unionism. It faced hostility from the traditionally male trade union movement, but Mary was undaunted. By the end of its first year, the NFWW had seventeen branches and around 2,000 members. By 1914 some 300,000 women were involved.

In 1910 Mary led women working as chainmakers in Cradley Heath in the Black Country to victory in a fight for a fair wage after a ten-week strike. In 1911 she returned to London and co-ordinated successful strikes by female factory workers in Bermondsey against starvation wages.

Will Anderson followed Mary to London in 1910 and the couple married in 1911. Their first child died at birth in 1913. In 1914, Will was elected to the House of Commons and in 1915 Mary gave birth to a daughter, Anne. In 1916 Mary joined the Government reconstruction committee, and after women over thirty received the vote in 1918, she stood for election but was defeated, along with others who opposed the First World War. Will, too, lost his seat. Some blamed Mary's defeat on the fact that the ballot paper named her as 'Mrs W.C. Anderson' when she was best known by her own name.

Neither of the Andersons had the chance to stand for election again. Will died in the 1919 influenza epidemic and in the following year Mary discovered she had terminal cancer. She died in 1921, at the age of just forty. On the day of her death her union merged with two others to form the National Union of General and Municipal Workers – today's GMB.

The *Woman Worker* magazine marked Mary's passing as the death of 'A Great Leader', while economist and social reformer Beatrice Webb described her as 'the axle round which the machinery moved'.

"While women are badly paid because of their unorganised condition, they remain unorganised mainly because they are badly paid."

MARY MACARTHUR

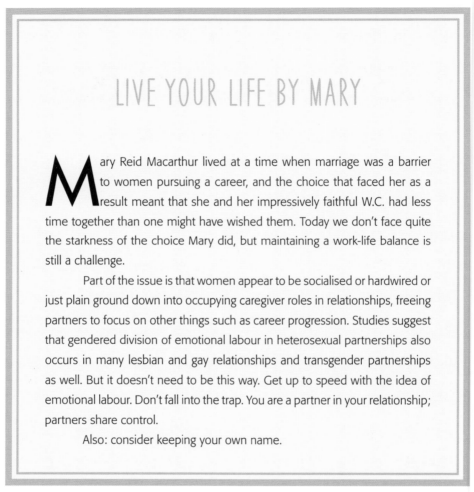

LIVE YOUR LIFE BY MARY

Mary Reid Macarthur lived at a time when marriage was a barrier to women pursuing a career, and the choice that faced her as a result meant that she and her impressively faithful W.C. had less time together than one might have wished them. Today we don't face quite the starkness of the choice Mary did, but maintaining a work-life balance is still a challenge.

Part of the issue is that women appear to be socialised or hardwired or just plain ground down into occupying caregiver roles in relationships, freeing partners to focus on other things such as career progression. Studies suggest that gendered division of emotional labour in heterosexual partnerships also occurs in many lesbian and gay relationships and transgender partnerships as well. But it doesn't need to be this way. Get up to speed with the idea of emotional labour. Don't fall into the trap. You are a partner in your relationship; partners share control.

Also: consider keeping your own name.

MARY BROOKSBANK
POET AND TRADE UNIONIST

Think you had it tough with your paper-round? By the age of twelve, Mary Brooksbank had been taken on as a 'shifter' in the Baltic Jute Mill in Dundee. Jute was a booming industry, and Mary's family had left the Aberdeen slum where she was born and moved south in the hope of getting in on the action. Unfortunately, jute was an exploitative industry, too, employing mainly women because they commanded lower wages than men, and subjecting them to hellish conditions.

By the age of fourteen, Mary was a trade unionist, marching with the other girls from her mill for a pay rise. They succeeded in securing a not insignificant 15 per cent. Her mother attempted to tame her with a wee spell 'in service', working as a maid for a wealthy family. Mary was having none of it. 'It was the worst thing she could have did,' she said. 'I saw right away the contrast between their homes and ours, you know, thons o the gentry and ours.'

Mary's early experiences in Dundee inspired her lifelong commitment to improving the conditions of working people. She joined the Communist Party and, despite her diminutive status, she was active in protests and demonstrations and was imprisoned for her actions on a number of occasions. Eventually she left the Party, unable to reconcile her membership with what was becoming known regarding the murderous actions of Josef Stalin. She attended classes run by socialist revolutionary John McLean in Glasgow and began to develop an interest in his vision of a Scottish 'socialist workers' republic'.

If politics was the one real touchstone in Mary's life, music was the way

"I have never had any personal ambitions. I have but one: to make my contribution to destroy the capitalist system."

MARY BROOKSBANK

she best made her views known. Her family had all been musical, and she could sing, play the fiddle and compose her own songs. She was even known to busk on the Dundee to Tayport ferry and in the street. To this day her 'Jute Mill Song' is sung in folk clubs across the country and has been recorded by Ewan MacColl and Peggy Seeger among many others. It was inspired by a conversation with another 'shifter' in the mills who was struggling to support her illegitimate child. 'O dear me,' Mary's song says, 'the world's ill divided. Them that works the hardest are aye wi' least provided.'

After Mary's death in 1978, Dundee named a library in her honour. The words of the 'Jute Mill Song' were the first woman's words – and the first communist's – to be quoted on the walls of the Scottish Parliament.

LIVE YOUR LIFE BY MARY

Mary said, 'We're the better of a sang.' She's right – singing involves breathing deeply and letting out a bit of tension and it has proven beneficial effects on our wellbeing. Chanting and humming are also good. Yoga practices such as *bhramari pranayama* (bee breath), are soothing for a spinning mind.

Try these things simply in and of themselves, and to help develop your voice. A strong voice is a great thing. Cherish it and don't ever be afraid to use it.

"I was a prisoner
on a snow-covered strip of
shingle about a mile long,
and scarcely in any part
more than a hundred yards
wide, washed on
all sides by the sea.
Escape – had I desired
it – was impossible."

ISOBEL WYLIE HUTCHISON
NORTH TO THE RIME-RINGED SUN
1934

ISOBEL WYLIE HUTCHISON

EXPLORER, WRITER AND BOTANIST

A journalist from *The Scotsman* visited Isobel Wylie Hutchison in 1939 and made the hilarious observation that she was 'much too fragile and gentle for the rigours of Arctic exploration'. The journalist might have been impressed by Isobel's dexterity with the teapot, but Isobel had long since decided that domesticity was not for her, marriage would restrict her ambitions, and no one would tell her what she could and couldn't do. She had also spent significant periods of time in some of the most inhospitable locations on Earth.

Isobel was born into a prosperous family in the rather comfortable Cairlowrie Castle in 1889. Her young life mixed the joyful – croquet and dancing, archery, tennis and long 'strolls' – with the desperately sad. Her father died when she was just ten, and she lost two brothers shortly thereafter. Young Isobel was a keen writer and fascinated by languages – during her life she learned Italian, Greek, Hebrew, Gaelic, Danish, Icelandic, Greenlandic and some Inuit. She began to enjoy some success as a writer relatively early in life, supplementing the trust fund her father had left her and supporting her lifelong wanderlust.

Isobel's first overseas travels took her to Spain, Morocco, Egypt and Israel, and when she returned to Scotland she trekked 150 miles from Barra to Lewis in the Western Isles. An article for *National Geographic Magazine* on this trip paid for a further journey to Iceland, where she travelled solo around the country on foot and horseback, much to the dismay of local guides.

Next on Isobel's list was Greenland, which was easier decided than done.

Denmark limited access at the time, but Isobel was able to obtain a visa to collect botanical specimens, an interest she had inherited from her father. While she was in the country, she shot some wonderful footage now held in the Scottish Screen Archive. It captures the Greenlanders' mastery of the country dances they had learned from Scottish whalers, and some on point seal-fur shorts. After a visit home, Isobel returned to the West Coast of Greenland for a stay of several months. She returned with dozens of plant specimens and her book *On Greenland's Closed Shore,* which brought her fame.

Alaska was next, and Isobel set off for the cold once more, collecting over two hundred plant specimens and staying among the Inuit. During this trip she saw the eerie sight of the SS *Baychimo*, a 'ghost ship' that had become trapped in ice and was slowly sailing, crewless, in the ice. Isobel being Isobel, she went on board and availed herself of some stationery to write a letter home.

Isobel carried on travelling for the rest of her life. She returned to the Arctic, and visited Japan, China, Russia, Poland, Germany, Estonia and Denmark. She was remained a keen walker and was still cycling long distances well into her later years.

LIVE YOUR LIFE BY ISOBEL

Isobel spent time travelling and staying with friends and contacts (sometimes UNCHAPERONED! with MEN!), but she was first and foremost a solo traveller and is reported to have said, 'I am glad to be alone.'

Not all of us are as comfortable in our own company, but this is a skill worth cultivating. Time spent alone allows us many things. It is a way to know ourselves better – being alone with our thoughts gives us the chance to reflect, to problem-solve and to think outside the box. It lets us focus on our needs and our development – self-care is easier when we don't have to eliminate other voices to hear our own. It is also a way to develop our creative powers – artists often use specially arranged retreats to dive into ideas, reach deep into their imaginations and produce new and experimental work. It's no coincidence that Isobel produced some brilliant writing during and after her periods of solitude.

Being alone is not about reading a book or browsing the net or watching a film or TV programme, but rather about making space with no distractions to spend time with your thoughts. You can do this in small ways – a walk, or a lunch break in your own company are good ways to start – or you might like to try larger commitments, such as a trip away alone. To really benefit, switch off your devices or leave them at home.

"Born in the lush tropics of the South Seas, she married a Fifer and came 10,000 miles across the world and ended her days in Anstruther, on the shores of the cold and stormy North Sea."

PRINCESS TITAUA MARAMA'S GRAVESTONE
ANSTRUTHER, FIFE

TETUANUI~REIA ~ITE~RAIATEA

CHIEFTESS

Next time you hear someone is expecting a baby girl, don't be afraid to recommend a strong name. Tetuanui-reia-ite-raiatea, for example, means the Great God Whose Power Extends to the Heavens.

Tetuanui-reia-ite-raiatea actually came by her Tahitian royal moniker a little later in life. She was originally named Titaua Marama, and was the eldest child born to Englishman Alexander Salmon and the sister of Queen Pomare the Fourth of Tahiti. Tahitian custom allowed for the Queen to adopt her sister's child, and that was the point at which Titaua received her fantastic new name.

When Titaua was just fourteen years old, she was married to a trader named John Brander, who originated in Elgin. Brander had significant wealth and power in the South Pacific and although to a modern mind Titaua's age at marriage provokes a shudder, the Princess owned the position her status and Brander's wealth gave her. She was the foremost hostess in Tahiti, welcoming illustrious visitors from across the globe, including Robert Louis Stevenson and Prince Alfred, son of Queen Victoria.

Tahiti was at the time a French colony, and the power of the Brander company caused the colonial administrators significant concerns there and in neighbouring territories (well, as neighbouring as the South Pacific allows). When Brander died in 1877, there may have been hopes that the company's influence would wane. Titaua had other ideas; she married again and continued to control

Maison Brander. Using Titaua's commercial networks and the family connections, the Tahitian royal family continued to develop their influence across the Pacific.

Titaua's second husband was George Darsie of Anstruther in Fife, an associate of her first husband. Titaua and George had three children, adding to the nine she already had from her first marriage. When George Darsie retired, he, Titaua and her five youngest children made the crossing from Tahiti to Scotland and moved into the Darsie family home, Johnston Lodge in Anstruther. Titaua it seems was popular among the locals and continued to welcome royal visitors from the other side of the world.

LIVE YOUR LIFE BY TITAUA

Titaua travelled the world, embraced a new community on the other side of the globe from home, and was embraced by them in turn. Her story is a complex one, involving colonial interactions and skewed power-structures, and richly divergent cultural contexts. She enriched Scotland at both a local level and a national one – her possessions form a key part of the National Museums' Pacific collections – and her story reminds us of the complexities and complicities in our history.

Let's honour Titaua, by making Scotland an open country where we are willing to face up to our past, and where we make reparations for the ugly actions in our history. Most importantly of all, let's make this a welcoming place for those who wish to build meaningful and sustainable lives here – our new Scots are part of our community, and part of the story of our future.

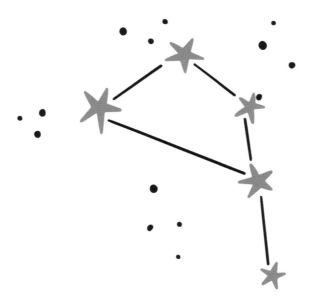

A WOMAN'S WORK
IS NEVER DONE

TAKEAWAYS

Choosing women for this book was not an easy task. For every woman with an inspiring, thought-provoking or troubling story told here, many more might have been included — and this is true even for those periods for which our records are scarcest.

Amy NicRuairidh's aunt Christina was a supporter of Robert Bruce, for example, active in clan politics and with opinions that frequently differed from those of the men around her. In the Lowlands around the same period, between the death of Isabella MacDuff and Black Agnes's heroic stand at Dunbar Castle, Christian, the wife of Governor Seton of Berwick, watched as her son Thomas was hanged before her eyes in an attempt to coerce her husband into surrendering to besieging forces. The Setons stood firm.

MARYS, MARGARETS AND ROYAL SERVANTS

In 1286, Margaret, Maid of Norway was named successor to her grandfather Alexander III but perished on her journey from the country of her birth before she could take up the throne. There is a bizarre postscript to her story in the case of 'False Margaret', an older woman who later claimed to be Margaret, and was burned at the stake in Bergen as punishment. Almost three hundred years would pass before another woman – Mary Stuart – was named queen in her own right, but of course Scotland had centuries' worth of queens consort whose stories are also worth the telling.

Eleventh-century religious reformer Saint Margaret is perhaps the most famous of these women, founder of the ferry across the Forth and Anglicising influence on the Scottish court. Another English Margaret, the child bride of Alexander III, initially appears a sympathetic character, writing to her parents in the 1250s to complain of homesickness, the Scottish climate and the absence of her beloved husband's affections since intimacy was forbidden between a ten- and an eleven-year-old. Later she absconds from Scotland in order to have her mother by her side as she gives birth to her first child. She tarnishes her reputation rather in the end by persuading a maid to push a courtier into the Tay for sport, whereupon the unfortunate man is swept away by the current and drowned, and Margaret much upset, as well she might be. She lived only a few years longer, dying at thirty-four.

The lifespan of Scottish kings was often similarly short – war, disease and downright bad luck took them off – and many dowager queens governed as regents during the minorities of their children. Mary of Guelders was one such in the 1400s, as was Margaret Tudor in the 1500s, followed shortly thereafter by her daughter-in-law Mary of Guise. This formidable French noblewoman was mother of Mary Queen of Scots, and brokered the French marriage that made her daughter doubly a queen.

Queens of course had their waiting women, of whom Mary Stuart's 'Four Maries' are remembered in a well-known song. Mary had other loyal women too, two of whom accompanied her to the very end, gently chastised by their mistress for weeping while she remained calm in the face of her fate. Catherine Douglas, or Kate Barlass, was made of sterner stuff. She was lady-in-waiting to Joan Beaufort, wife of King James I, and was in her own right a cousin to the king. James was staying in a monastic house in Perth in 1437 when a group of men came to kill him. Legend has it that the King's Chamberlain, in on the plan, had removed the heavy bolt from the door of the royal couple's chamber to facilitate easy access for the assassins. Catherine placed her arm through the staples of the door while James fled into a sewer and the queen and her other ladies scrambled to hide his escape route from view. It was to no avail – the assassins forced the door open anyway, breaking Catherine's arm in the process, and killed the king.

(Should you fancy your chances as a modern-day royal servant, HM the Queen occasionally advertises for maids for her Scottish residence, where you can earn the fabulous wage of £12,000 a year.)

THE SPIRIT OF DISSENT

Mary Stuart's son James's witch trials are a stain on Scotland's history and, as noted before, far too many women's names appear in those records that survive. Religious persecution, too, was meted out extensively to women, especially during the Covenanting period when women became key players in the crucial venture of the new faith.

Alongside the names of Margarets Wilson and McLachlan, Isabel Alison and many more lost their lives, but many more still survived to take an active role in campaigning and dissent, building on Jenny Geddes's legacy – real or legendary – to establish a firm tradition of female activism that survives in Scotland into the present day. Here, perhaps, are the roots of the campaigning of Flora Drummond, the Wighams, Chrystal MacMillan, Jessie Craigen, Helen Crawfurd, Mary Barbour, Ethel MacDonald, Helen Crummy, Maggie Keswick Jencks and many, many more. Perhaps even the roots of Janey Godley and her 'Trump is a cunt' sign.

This spirit is firmly in view in the various rebellions of the 17th and 18th centuries, when Jacobitism in particular gives us a slew of women demonstrating their loyalty and courage. Here Isabella Lumsden spins and sings while redcoat soldiers search her house for the lover hidden in her petticoats; there Mrs Murray of Broughton rides into Edinburgh alongside her husband in the Jacobite army with a naked blade on her thighs. One Margaret Ogilvy holds her husband's horse at the battles of Falkirk and Culloden and escapes from Edinburgh Castle dressed as a washerwoman.

OUR GAELIC FOREMOTHERS

Jacobite women's tradition doesn't of course always tell of such good outcomes. A number of women poets in the Gaelic tradition leave us accounts of their devastation as the various military campaigns and reprisals thereafter rob them of husbands, children, friends and land.

Christina Ferguson, widow of William Chisholm of Strathglass, is one of these. 'Oh young Charles Stuart,' she says, 'your cause has been my destruction.' Sìleas, daughter of Archibald MacDonald of Keppoch, is best known for a number of elegant Jacobite-themed works, including her famous, tearing lament for Alasdair of Glengarry, 'rogha nan darag as àirde', the *best of the tallest oaks*. Poor Sìleas had other reasons to lament too; tradition has it that her husband died after choking on a glass of claret.

Without the stories of our Gaelic foremothers, we cannot give a full account of Scotland's women, and yet these voices are often excluded for the simple reason that their words do not yet exist in translation, and few of us can understand them in the original. Without Gaelic we miss out on the warrior women of legend, the queens of Alba and the holy women of the west coast. Much of early poetry is closed to us – Iseabal Ní Mheic Cailein's boast on the size and potency of her household priest's penis might cause you to reassess the fun to be had in the 1400s – as is much of the Jacobite women's tradition. There are also gems such as the song composed by the foster mother of Donald Mac Iain 'ic Sheumais of Clanranald as she drew an arrow from his thigh at the battle of Carinish in 1601, and stopped the bleeding with her own mouth.

IN MY SKIN

The Gaelic tradition, of course, offers a rich vein of anonymous women's voices that speak with crystal clarity through the centuries:

> Gur i saighead na h-àraich
> Seo thàrmaich am leathar.
>
> Chaidh saighead am shliasaid,
> Crann fiar air dhroch shnaidheadh.

> *An arrow from this battle*
> *has lodged in my skin.*
>
> *An arrow went into my thigh*
> *a bent shaft, badly carved.*

It's #MeToo, 1500s style.

The question of language is worth noting; we would, of course, struggle to converse with many of the women in this book should some magic trick of time allow us to meet them. Some spoke older varieties of English or historical variants of Gaelic or Scots, and many of their words and deeds are preserved in Latin, Early Scottish Gaelic and centuries-old French. Those who wrote did so in a still broader range of languages and language variants.

OUR VOICES THAT TELL STORIES

Writing – in whatever language – has been a talent of Scotland's for centuries and our Scottish women writers are far, far too many to list.

From the modern era – relatively speaking – only Naomi Mitchison is here, but where would we be without Muriel Spark, Violet Jacob, Marion Angus, Liz Lochhead, Jessie Kesson, Val Gillies, Jackie Kay, Janice Galloway, Ali Smith, Val McDermid . . . The list goes on. The further back we reach, the more our female writers have tended to be forgotten. Susan Ferrier, Margaret Oliphant, Joanna Bailey, Susan Edmonstone, Mary Brunton, Catherine Sinclair, Josephine Tey, Willa Muir, Nancy Brysson Morrison, Alison Cockburn, Marjorie Fleming, Elizabeth Melville, Janet Hamilton, Anne Grant, Lady Anne Barnard and many more have slipped from print and from memory.

Nan Shepherd has recently enjoyed something of a renaissance thanks to the publisher Canongate; hopefully more female voices will find their way back into print or otherwise to a readership via other dissemination mechanisms. Projects such as Tobar an Dualchais/Kist o' Riches and the digitisation work of the National Library of Scotland has already begun to make more voices available to us – Belle Stewart can be heard extensively in the former, along with hundreds of other singers, storytellers and recounters of lived history.

As well as our storytellers in the written and spoken word, Scotland had and has many women painters, actors, filmmakers and other artists, from Orkney's pioneering Margaret Tait in her 'lonely furrow' to the 2018 Turner Prize winner Charlotte Prodger. We've seen pioneers in sport, too, from early golfers in Violet Henry-Anderson, Elsie Grant Suttie and many more, to modern-day sports campaigner Judy Murray. Our runners in particular have shown that women don't always have to 'choose'. Liz McColgan made a famous return from maternity leave to competition in the 1990s, and Jasmin Paris paused in the 2019 Montane Spine Race to express milk – and still smashed the record for the wintry 268-mile race.

We have business women – Bessie Millar might have been proud, or Janet Keiller, who first brought orange marmalade to market in 1797 – and women ministers, recalling the faith-based sacrifice of Jane Haining and the work of other missionaries including Mary Slessor. Our government in 2019 has a gender-balanced cabinet, across the political spectrum female party leaders are no longer an exception, and we have a tradition of strong female voices in both Edinburgh and Westminster, following in the fine tradition of Jennie Lee.

FINDING INSPIRATION

The aim of this book has been to inspire, intrigue and entertain. It is intended to be accessible to anyone, and its portraits by necessity consist of the briefest of snapshots of particular points in these women's lives. Its aim is not, however, to simplify, to reduce these women to poster girls or their words to shareable quotes. Each of them was a human being, with all of the complexity and contradiction that implies. While the book seeks to find inspiration in each of their lives, no one is claiming that this is inspiration they would recognise. Their times were not our times and their thoughts, their values and standards were not ours. They may have viewed their stories very differently; indeed they might not recognise these portraits at all.

The last words in this book are for the countless women whose stories have gone unrecorded over the centuries. Fishwives and herring gutters, farm quines and dairy maids, coalhowkers and millworkers, knitters and sewers and weavers and washerwomen, cooks and cleaners, teachers and bank clerks and bus-drivers and shop assistants and administrators and pharmacists and midwives and doctors and nurses; mothers, daughters, widows, lovers and friends in their millions. Their threads are the ground of our history, the warp and the weft of the fabric of Scotland. This book is for them.

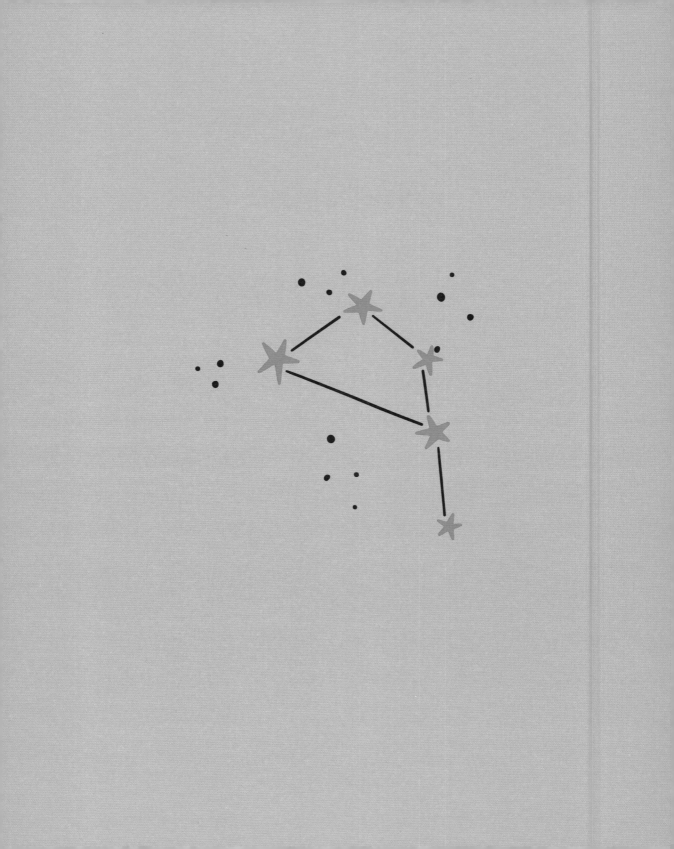

TAING
THANKS

Books are a team effort, and my first thanks go to Campbell and Ali, Janne, Jaz, Thomas, Tonje and all at Black & White, who gamely took on a rather different book from the one first mooted over a coffee many (many!) months previously. Special thanks to Alice for all of her kind editorial attention (and Latin advice) and to Emma Hargrave for her meticulous, thoughtful and caring attention to every warrior, witch and damn rebel bitch. She is herself the best of women, and the kindest of friends.

Many people were generous with time, expertise and enthusiasm. Special thanks are due to Abigail Burnyeat for helping me find Sgàthach's *Imbas Forosnai* and to Dòmhnall Uilleam Stiùbhart for advice on another Gaelic source when I was struggling. Jenny Niven championed the inclusion of Devorgilla, Joan Parr the quiet voices, and Kirsty MacDonald her distant relative Isobel Wylie Hutchison. Many other friends and family members suggested women for inclusion, and were kind enough not to take it on the nose if I couldn't fit them in.

I'm the daughter of historians who kept me right as I wrote – any errors are, of course, mine – and I am so grateful to them for all they have given me. I will always be grateful too to the (other) gifted, kind and knowledgeable teachers who first introduced me to a love of story, of writing and of history – Mary Linton, Judy Hayman, Douglas Robb and Margot Alexander in particular – and to Ronnie Black, Willie Gillies, Allan MacDonald and Rob Mullally, who gave me my enduring love of the literature, lore and poetry of the Gaelic tradition. I checked layouts of the book just as we said goodbye to the late, great John MacInnes and my love and thoughts are with Catrìona, Sinead and the rest of his family in their loss.

Biggest thanks of all go to Tom Morgan-Jones, best and most patient of husbands, who listened to and read more drafts of the stories in this book than anyone should have to bear. You're the best, my love. *Hello!*

MAIRI KIDD is a writer, publisher and translator who works by day to support the world of Scottish books and reading as Head of Literature at Creative Scotland. Her previous work includes BAFTA-nominated BBC drama *Eilbheas* (co-written with Torcuil Crichton), an edition of traditional stories for children, and the world's first Gaelic translation of *Oor Wullie*.

Mairi lives in Edinburgh, and sleeps in the self-same room in which Rachel Chiesley was born in the late 17th century. Legend has it it's haunted; she doesn't believe it.